For usage rights and other information pertaining to this
publication contact:

Wall Street Prep, Inc.
Tel: 800-646-3575
Email: info@wallstreetprep.com
Website address: www.wallstreetprep.com

Welcome

Welcome to Wall Street Prep's *Crash Course in Accounting & Financial Statement Analysis.*

This is an exercise-based guide designed to efficiently provide students and professionals who are pursuing a career in finance with practical, real-world accounting and financial statement analysis skills.

Accordingly, this book also serves as the groundwork for those who intend to proceed with more rigorous financial training involving financial and valuation modeling.

Good luck,

Matan Feldman
Wall Street Prep, Inc.

Arkady Libman
Wall Street Prep, Inc.

About Wall Street Prep

WALL STREET *PREP*
FINANCIAL TRAINING SOLUTIONS

www.WallStreetPrep.com
Toll-free: (800) 646 3575

Wall Street Prep Inc. was established by investment bankers to equip students and professionals with practical, real-world financial skills.

Wall Street Prep's renowned step-by-step self-study courses, and customized university and corporate training seminars cover the areas of Financial Accounting, Corporate Finance, Excel, Financial Modeling, Valuation Modeling, and Mergers & Acquisitions (M&A) Modeling.

Self-study programs available online

Step-by-Step Financial Modeling

*   Simulate on-the-job financial modeling using our tutorial materials and Excel model templates.
*   Build, understand, analyze, and interpret complex financial earnings models.
*   Step-by-step instructions on building projections of financial statements.

Step-by-Step Advanced Valuation Modeling

*   Learn Discounted Cash Flow (DCF) modeling, Leveraged Buyout (LBO) analysis, M&A analysis, comparable company analysis ("Comps"), and comparable transaction analysis.
*   Step-by-step instruction on building, understanding, analyzing, and interpreting applications of traditional valuation methodologies the way it is done in the finance industry.

TABLE OF CONTENTS

TABLE OF CONTENTS

CHAPTER 1

INTRODUCTION TO ACCOUNTING

WHAT IS ACCOUNTING?

➔ Accounting is the language of business. It is a standard set of rules for measuring a firm's financial performance. Assessing a company's financial performance is important for many groups, including:

- ☑ The firm's officers (managers and employees)
- ☑ Investors (current and potential shareholders)
- ☑ Lenders (banks)
- ☑ General public

➔ Standard financial statements serve as a "yardstick" of communicating financial performance to the general public.

➔ For example, monthly sales volumes released by McDonald's Corp. provide both its managers and the general public with an opportunity to assess the company's financial performance across major geographic segments (U.S., Europe, Asia Pacific, Middle East, and Africa).

WHY IS ACCOUNTING IMPORTANT?

➔ **Making corporate decisions**
Suppose a telecom company is looking to acquire a regional company to boost its presence in that region. There are several potential targets that fit the bill. How does this company determine which of these, if any, companies would make a good acquisition candidate?

➔ **Making investment decisions**
A mutual fund is looking to invest in several diverse technology companies – Microsoft, Oracle, and Intel. How does this mutual fund determine in which of these, if any, companies it should make an investment?

➔ A major part of corporate and investment decisions relies on analyzing each of the companies' financial information in the above-mentioned cases.

➔ Accounting, the standard language by which such financial information can be assessed and compared, is fundamental to making these decisions.

➜ Accounting is used by a variety of organizations – from the federal government to non-profit organizations to small businesses to corporations.

➜ We will be discussing accounting rules as they pertain to publicly-traded companies.

Figure 1. Who uses accounting?

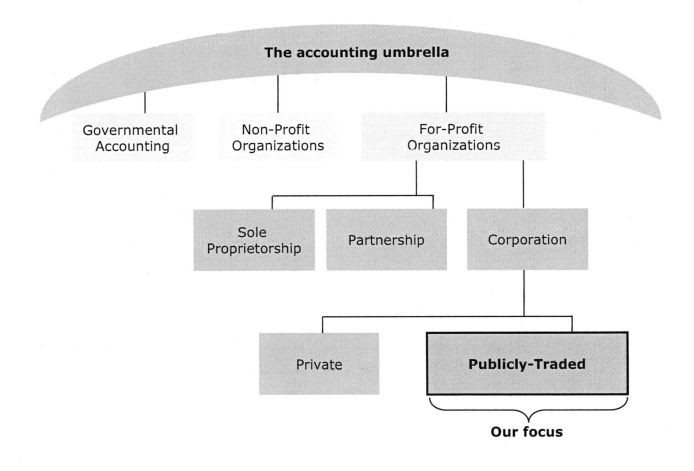

ACCOUNTING REGULATIONS

➜ Accounting attempts to standardize financial information, and like any language, follows rules and regulations. What are these accounting rules, how are they established, and by whom?

Generally Accepted Accounting Principles (GAAP)

➜ A governmental agency called the Securities and Exchange Commission (SEC) authorizes the Financial Accounting Standards Board (FASB) to determine U.S. accounting rules.

➜ FASB communicates these rules through the issuance of Statements of Financial Accounting Standards (SFAS). These statements make up the body of accounting rules known as the Generally Accepted Accounting Principles (GAAP).

➜ These rules have been developed to provide guidelines for financial accounting in order to ensure that businesses present their financial information in a fair, consistent, and straight-forward basis. Financial statements must be prepared according to GAAP.

AN OVERVIEW OF THE SEC

➜ The Securities and Exchange Commission is a U.S. federal agency, which was established by the U.S. Congress in 1934.

➜ The agency's primary mission is "to protect investors and maintain the integrity of the securities markets," which includes the establishment and maintenance of accounting principles and regulations.

➜ The SEC is comprised of five presidentially-appointed Commissioners heading approximately 3,100 staff employees across 4 Divisions and 18 Offices.

Figure 2. SEC organizational structure

	Securities & Exchange Commission (SEC) Five Presidentially-Appointed Commissioners 3,100 staff and 18 Offices			
Divisions	**Division of Corporate Finance**	**Division of Market Regulation**	**Division of Investment Management**	**Division of Enforcement**
Major Oversight	Oversees financial reporting by corporations; Monitors the activities of FASB	Establishes and maintains market rules through regulation of stock exchanges and broker-dealers	Regulates investment companies and investment advisers	Oversees securities laws violations (insider trading, securities price manipulation, etc.)

AN OVERVIEW OF FASB

➜ The SEC has historically designated the private sector with establishing and maintaining financial accounting and reporting standards. Accordingly, the Financial Accounting Standards Board (FASB) was established in 1973 to carry out these functions on the behalf of the SEC.

➜ FASB is composed of seven full-time members appointed for five years by the Financial Accounting Foundation (FAF), a "parent" organization.

➜ FASB formulates accounting standards through the issuance of Statements of Financial Accounting Standards (SFAS). These statements make up the body of accounting rules known as the Generally Accepted Accounting Principles (GAAP).

➜ While the FASB is independent, with close relations with the SEC, its decisions are influenced by a variety of entities.

Figure 3. FASB receives input from a variety of sources

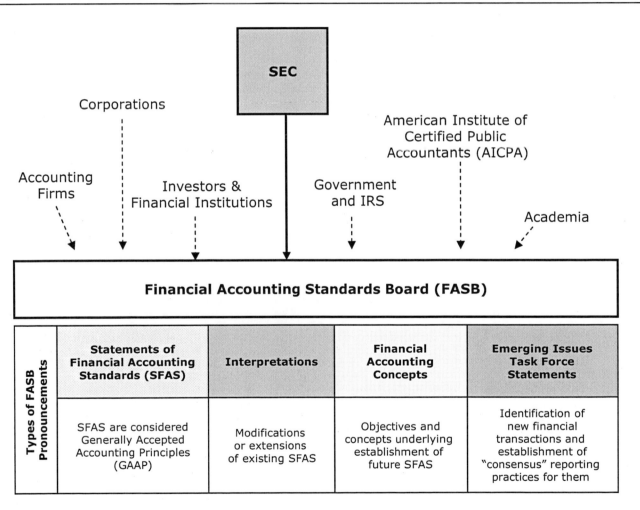

Types of FASB Pronouncements	Statements of Financial Accounting Standards (SFAS)	Interpretations	Financial Accounting Concepts	Emerging Issues Task Force Statements
	SFAS are considered Generally Accepted Accounting Principles (GAAP)	Modifications or extensions of existing SFAS	Objectives and concepts underlying establishment of future SFAS	Identification of new financial transactions and establishment of "consensus" reporting practices for them

GAAP VARY ACROSS DIFFERENT COUNTRIES

→ Although GAAP vary from country to country, there has been unprecedented convergence of international accounting standards over the last few years.

→ By 2005, all European companies will report under International Financial Reporting Standards (IFRS) – formerly IAS. Accounting standards for many countries outside of Europe - including Japan - are largely equivalent to IFRS.

→ There remain some differences between U.S. GAAP and IFRS, and where those differences exist, this course presumes U.S. GAAP.

→ Log on to www.wallstreetprep.com/accounting.html for a list of major differences.

SUMMARY

➔ Accounting is a standard language of measuring financial performance by a variety of organizations.

➔ Accounting follows Generally Accepted Accounting Principles (GAAP), which are guidelines for measuring and presenting financial information in a fair, consistent, and straight-forward basis.

➔ U.S. GAAP are developed by FASB on the behalf of the SEC, with input from a variety of interest groups.

➔ Although we have seen unprecedented convergence over the last few years of GAAP among different countries, there remain some differences.

CHAPTER 2

BASIC ACCOUNTING PRINCIPLES

ASSUMPTIONS, PRINCIPLES, AND CONSTRAINTS

➜   Generally Accepted Accounting Principles have been established as a way to standardize the presentation of financial information.

➜   FASB attempts to base GAAP on several key theoretical assumptions, principles, and constraints. They are introduced here and will be revisited in further detail throughout the book.

ASSUMPTION #1: ACCOUNTING ENTITY

➜   A company is considered a separate "living" enterprise, apart from its owners. In other words, a corporation is a "fictional" being – it has a name as well as a birth date and birth place (referred to as incorporation date and place, respectively); it is engaged in clearly-defined activities; regularly reports its financial health (through financial reports) to the general public; pays taxes; and can file lawsuits.

ASSUMPTION #2: GOING CONCERN

➜   A company is considered viable and a "going concern" for the foreseeable future. In other words, a corporation is assumed to remain in existence for an indefinitely long time. ExxonMobil, for example, has existed since 1882, and General Electric has been around since 1892 – both of these companies are expected to continue to operate in the future.

Advanced Discussion:
Why assume "going concern"?

⤷   To assume that an entity will continue to remain in business is fundamental to accounting for publicly-held companies.

⤷   The going concern assumption essentially says that a company expects to continue operating indefinitely; that is, it expects to realize its assets at the recorded amounts and to extinguish its liabilities in the normal course of business.

⤷   If this assumption is incorrect or untenable for a particular company, then the methods prescribed by GAAP for accounting for various transactions would need to be adjusted, with consequences to revenues, expenses, and equity.

ASSUMPTION #3: MEASUREMENT

➔ Financial statements have limitations – they show only measurable activities of a corporation such as its quantifiable resources, its liabilities (money owed by it), amount of taxes facing it, etc. For example, financial statements exclude:

⇨ Internally-developed trademarks and patents (think of Coke, Microsoft, GE) – the value of these brands cannot be quantified and therefore recorded.

⇨ Employee and customer loyalty – their value is undeterminable.

➔ Since financial statements show only measurable activities of a company, they must be reported in the national monetary unit. U.S. financial statements are reported in U.S. dollars; many European financial statements use Euro as a monetary unit.

Figure 4. Financial statements of U.S. companies are reported in U.S. dollars

ExxonMobil 2004 10-K

CONSOLIDATED STATEMENT OF INCOME

	Note Reference Number	2004	2003	2002
		(millions of dollars)		
Revenues and other income				
Sales and other operating revenue [1]		$291,252	$237,054	$200,949
Income from equity affiliates	7	4,961	4,373	2,066
Other income		1,822	5,311	1,491
Total revenues and other income		$298,035	$246,738	$204,506
Costs and other deductions				
Crude oil and product purchases		$139,224	$107,658	$ 90,950
Production and manufacturing expenses		23,225	21,260	17,831
Selling, general and administrative expenses		13,849	13,396	12,356
Depreciation and depletion		9,767	9,047	8,310
Exploration expenses, including dry holes		1,098	1,010	920
Merger-related expenses	3	—	—	410
Interest expense		638	207	398
Excise taxes [1]	19	27,263	23,855	22,040
Other taxes and duties	19	40,954	37,645	33,572
Income applicable to minority and preferred interests		776	694	209
Total costs and other deductions		$256,794	$214,772	$186,996
Income before income taxes		$ 41,241	$ 31,966	$ 17,510
Income taxes	19	15,911	11,006	6,499
Income from continuing operations		$ 25,330	$ 20,960	$ 11,011
Discontinued operations, net of income tax	2	—	—	449
Cumulative effect of accounting change, net of income tax		—	550	—
Net income		$ 25,330	$ 21,510	$ 11,460
Net income per common share *(dollars)*	12			
Income from continuing operations		$ 3.91	$ 3.16	$ 1.62
Discontinued operations, net of income tax		—	—	0.07
Cumulative effect of accounting change, net of income tax		—	0.08	—
Net income		$ 3.91	$ 3.24	$ 1.69
Net income per common share – assuming dilution *(dollars)*	12			
Income from continuing operations		$ 3.89	$ 3.15	$ 1.61
Discontinued operations, net of income tax		—	—	0.07
Cumulative effect of accounting change, net of income tax		—	0.08	—
Net income		$ 3.89	$ 3.23	$ 1.68

ASSUMPTION #4: PERIODICITY

➜ A continuous life of an entity can be divided into measured periods of time, for which financial statements are prepared.

➜ U.S. companies are required to file quarterly (10-Q) and annual (10-K) financial reports.

➜ Typically one calendar year represents one accounting year (usually referred to as a fiscal year) for a company.

➜ Be aware that while many corporations align their fiscal years with calendar years, others do not:
- ⇨ ExxonMobil and General Electric have December 31st as their fiscal year-end.
- ⇨ Microsoft has June 30th and Wal-Mart, January 31st.

WRAP-UP

➜ We just covered 4 underlying assumptions in accounting:
1. Accounting Entity
2. Going Concern
3. Measurement
4. Periodicity

➜ We now turn to the major underlying accounting principles

BASIC ACCOUNTING PRINCIPLES

PRINCIPLE #1: HISTORICAL COST

➔   Financial statements report companies' resources at an initial historical cost.

➔   Let's assume a company purchased a piece of land for $1 million ten years ago. Under GAAP, it will continue to record this original purchase price (typically called book value) even though the market value (referred to as fair value) of this land has risen to $10 million.

➔   Why is such undervaluation of a company's resources required?

⇨   It represents the easiest measurement method without the need for constant appraisal and revaluation.

⇨   Just imagine the considerable amount of effort and subjectivity required to determine the fair value of all of General Electric's resources (plants, facilities, land) every year?

⇨   Additionally, marking resources up to fair value allows for management discretion and subjectivity, which GAAP attempts to minimize by using historical cost.

PRINCIPLES #2 and #3: ACCRUAL BASIS

➔   Accrual basis of accounting is one of the most important concepts in accounting, and governs the company's timing in recording its revenues (i.e. sales) and associated expenses.

⇨   **Principle #2: Revenue Recognition:** Accrual basis of accounting dictates that revenues must be recorded when earned <u>and</u> measurable.

⇨   **Principle #3: Matching Principle:** Under the matching principle, costs associated with making a product must be recorded during the same period as revenue generated from that product.

BASIC ACCOUNTING PRINCIPLES

Exercise: Amazon.com sells a book

The following transactions occurred on the specified dates:

1. Amazon.com purchases a book from a publisher for $10 on 6/5/03
2. Amazon.com receives a $20 credit card order for that book on 12/29/04
3. The book is shipped to customer on 1/4/05
4. Amazon.com receives cash on 2/1/05

From the options above, when should Amazon.com record revenue? Expenses?

Solution: Amazon.com sells a book

In line with the accrual principles of accounting, Amazon.com will record $20 in revenues and $10 in expenses on 1/4/05.

1. Amazon.com purchases a book from a publisher for $10 on 6/5/03
2. Amazon.com receives a $20 credit card order for that book on 12/29/04
3. **The book is shipped to customer on 1/4/05**
4. Amazon.com receives cash on 2/1/05

Why can't companies immediately record these revenues and expenses?

➜ According to the revenue recognition principle, a company cannot record revenue until that order is shipped to a customer (only then, is the revenue actually earned) and collection from that customer, who used a credit card, is reasonably assured.

Why shouldn't Amazon.com record the expense when it actually bought the book?

➜ According to the matching principle, costs associated with the production of the book should be recorded in (matched to) the same period as the revenue from the book's sale.

PRINCIPLE #4: FULL DISCLOSURE

➜ Under the full disclosure principle, companies must reveal all relevant economic information that they determine to make a difference to its users.

➜ Such disclosure should be accomplished in the following sections of companies' reports:

⇨ Financial statements
⇨ Notes to financial statements
⇨ Supplementary information

WRAP-UP

➜ We just covered 4 underlying principles in accounting:

1. Historical Cost
2. Accrual Accounting: Revenue Recognition
3. Accrual Accounting: Matching Principle
4. Full Disclosure

➜ We now turn to the major underlying accounting constraints

CONSTRAINT #1: ESTIMATES AND JUDGMENTS

→ Certain measurements cannot be performed completely accurately, and must therefore utilize conservative estimates and judgments.

→ For example, a company cannot fully predict the amount of money it will not collect from its customers, who having purchased goods from it on credit, ultimately decide not to pay. Instead, a company must make a conservative estimate based on its past experience with "bad" customers.

CONSTRAINT #2: MATERIALITY

→ Inclusion and disclosure of financial transactions in financial statements hinge on their size and effect on the company performing them.

→ Note that materiality varies across different entities – a material transaction (taking out a $1,000 loan) for a local lemonade stand is likely immaterial for General Electric, whose financial information is reported in billions of dollars.

CONSTRAINT #3: CONSISTENCY

→ For each company, the preparation of financial statements must utilize measurement techniques and assumptions which are consistent from one period to another.

→ As we will learn later in this book, companies can choose among several different accounting methods to measure the monetary value of their inventories. What matters is that a company consistently applies the same inventory method across different fiscal years.

CONSTRAINT #4: CONSERVATISM

→ Financial statements should be prepared with a downward measurement bias. Assets and revenues should not be overstated, while liabilities and expenses should not be understated.

→ Let's return to the historical cost principle, which requires a company to record the value of its resources at its original cost even if the current fair market value is considerably higher. Accordingly, the historical cost principle is an example of conservatism – assets are not allowed to be overstated.

BASIC ACCOUNTING PRINCIPLES

SUMMARY OF ACCOUNTING ASSUMPTIONS, PRINCIPLES, CONSTRAINTS

Accounting Entity	A corporation is considered a "living" enterprise i.e. a "fictional" being.
Going Concern	A corporation is assumed to remain in existence for the foreseeable future.
Measurement &	Financial statements show only measurable activities of a company.
Units of Measure	Financial statements must be reported in the national monetary unit (U.S. $ for U.S. companies).
Periodicity	A company's continuous life can be divided into measured periods of time for which financial statements are prepared. U.S. companies are required to file quarterly (10-Q) and annual (10-K) reports.
Historical Cost	Financial statements report companies' resources and obligations at an initial historical cost. This conservative measure precludes constant appraisal and revaluation.
Revenue Recognition	Revenues must be recorded when earned and measurable.
Matching Principle	Costs of a product must be recorded during the same period as revenue from selling it.
Disclosure	Companies must reveal all relevant economic information determined to make a difference to its users.
Estimates & Judgments	Certain measurements cannot be performed completely accurately, and must therefore utilize conservative estimates and judgments.
Materiality	Inclusion of certain financial transaction in financial statements hinges on their size and that of a company performing them.
Consistency	For each company, preparation of financial statements must utilize measurement techniques and assumptions which are consistent from one reporting period to another.
Conservatism	A downward measurement bias is used in the preparation of financial statements. Assets and revenues should not be overstated while liabilities and expenses should not be understated.

CHAPTER 3

FINANCIAL REPORTING

FINANCIAL REPORTING OVERVIEW

➜ Financial information, which accounting helps to standardize, is presented in the companies' financial reports.

➜ Companies must file periodic financial reports with the SEC – why?

"The laws and rules that govern the securities industry in the United States derive from a simple and straightforward concept: all investors, whether large institutions or private individuals, should have access to certain basic facts about an investment prior to buying it.

To achieve this, the SEC requires public companies to disclose meaningful financial and other information to the public, which provides a common pool of knowledge for all investors to use to judge for themselves if a company's securities are a good investment.

Only through the steady flow of timely, comprehensive and accurate information can people make sound investment decisions."

- Securities and Exchange Commission

FINDING FINANCIAL REPORTS

All filings made with the SEC constitute public information and can be found on:

1. The SEC's official website – http://www.sec.gov

2. Company websites – investor relations section

3. Electronic Data Gathering, Analysis, and Retrieval (EDGAR) website – http://www.freeedgar.com

FORM 10-K (ANNUAL FILING)

At the end of each fiscal year, publicly-traded companies must file a 10-K report which includes a thorough overview of their businesses and finances as well as their financial statements.

10-K's have historically been due 90 days after the close of companies' fiscal year. However, the SEC has shortened this period to 75 days (starting on 12/15/04) and to 60 days (starting on 12/15/05).

Why is the 10-K important?

→ Companies are required by the SEC to file it every year.

→ 10-K usually provides the most detailed overview of companies' financial operations and regulations governing them.

Annual Report vs. 10-K

In addition to a 10-K, at the end of each year companies also issue an Annual Report which contains management discussion, financial information, and data quite similar to a 10-K, and is sometimes confused with a 10-K.

However, an annual report is NOT the same as a 10-K.

An annual report is NOT a required SEC filing, and companies have a considerable amount of latitude in the structure and contents of this report.

While the Annual Report may contain details not reported elsewhere, in general, the 10-K presents a more detailed and unfettered picture of the company's operations and situation than is found in its regular annual report.

FORM 10-Q (QUARTERLY FILING)

At the end of each quarter of their fiscal year, publicly-traded companies also file a report with the SEC which includes financial statements and non-financial data.

10-Q's have historically been due 45 days after the close of companies' fiscal year. However, the SEC has shortened this period to 40 days (starting on 12/15/04) and to 35 days (starting on 12/15/05).

10-K vs. 10-Q – what's the difference?

10-Q financial reports are filed at the end of every quarter (for the first three quarters of a fiscal year); 10-K, at the end of each fiscal year.

While 10-K's and 10-Q's include financial statements, important footnotes and management commentary on the state of the business, 10-K's are generally more detailed filings than 10-Q's and contain valuable financial, company-specific, and industry information. Details regarding stock options, detailed debt schedules, and detailed financial footnotes should all be reviewed carefully.

10-K's (or Annual Reports) include extensive management commentary on the state of the business (management discussion & analysis "MD&A") and possibly include forward guidance.

10-K reports are reviewed by an independent auditor (a third party), while 10-Q filings are unaudited. This is important because an auditing firm may sometimes highlight certain financial information and valuation methodologies it believes do not conform with GAAP.

OTHER IMPORTANT FILINGS

Form 8-K

An 8-K is a required filing any time a company undergoes or announces a materially significant event such as an acquisition, a disposal of assets, bankruptcy, etc.

Form 14A

Form 14A is a required filing prior to companies' annual shareholder meetings. It contains detailed information about top officers and their compensations. The form often solicits shareholder votes (proxies) for Board nominees and other important matters.

SUMMARY OF OTHER FINANCIAL REPORTS

13-D: Tender Offers/Acquisition Reports	A 13-D by must be filed by 5%-or-more equity owners within 10 days of acquisition.
Related: 14D-1, SC 14D-1	14D-1 is submitted to the SEC at the same time as tender offer is made to holders of the equity securities of the target company.
C 13-G,13-G, SC 13-D	13-G must be filed by reporting persons (mainly institutions) with more than 5% ownership within 45 days after the end of the calendar year.
14-A: Proxies	14A is notification to shareholders of matters to be brought before shareholders meeting. It solicits proxy.
Related: 14C, Pre 14A, PRE 14C	14C is notification to shareholders of matters to be brought before shareholders meeting, but does not solicit proxy.
S-1: Registrations (Offering)	S-1 registration filed by a company when it decides to go "public" and sell securities. Known as an IPO (Initial Public Offering).
Related: S-2	S-2 filed to register a securities offering by companies meeting certain reporting requirements.
S-3	S-3 filed to register a securities offering by companies meeting certain reporting requirements and also certain requirements related to voting stock.
S-4	S-4 filed to register a securities offering in certain business combinations or reorganization.
S-11	S-11 Filed by real estate companies, mostly limited partnership and investment trusts.
10: Registrations (Trading)	10-12B and 10-12B/A are general registration filings of securities pursuant to section 12(b) of the SEC Act.
Related: 8-A, 8-A12B	8-A is a filing used to register additional securities or classes of securities.
8-B, 8-B12B	8-B: Used by successor issues – generally companies that have changed their name or state of incorporation – as notification that previously registered securities are to be traded under a new corporate identity.
20F	20-F: Registration/annual report filed by certain foreign issuers of securities trading in the U.S.
424A: Prospectuses	When the sale of securities is proposed in an offering registration statement, changes required by the SEC are incorporated into the Prospectus.
10-C	Report by issuer of securities quoted on NASDAQ interdealer quotation system, pursuant to section 13 or 15(d)
11-K	Annual report of employee stock purchase plans, savings and similar. Pursuant to rule 13a-10 or 15d-10
18-K	Annual report for foreign governments and political subdivisions

CHAPTER 4

READING THE ANNUAL REPORT

INTRODUCTION

➔ Truly the best way to begin getting a good grasp of how financial reports are organized and structured is simply by looking through them. Annual reports follow a fairly common structure:

- ⇨ Letter to Stockholders

- ⇨ Financial Highlights

- ⇨ Management's Discussion & Analysis (MD&A)

- ⇨ Financial Statements

- ⇨ Notes to Consolidated Statements

- ⇨ Report of Management's Responsibilities

- ⇨ Risk Factors

- ⇨ Legal Proceedings

- ⇨ Report of Independent Auditors

- ⇨ Directors & Officers

LETTER TO STOCKHOLDERS

➜ Usually at the start of an annual report, the Letter to Stockholders is written by top company officer(s). The letter summarizes major achievements during the year and provides highlights of strategic initiatives currently taking place.

➜ Letter to Stockholders can be regarded as a company's marketing piece. While certain financial milestones are mentioned, the emphasis is typically on a company's overall strategy and long-term goals.

Figure 5. Letter to stockholders

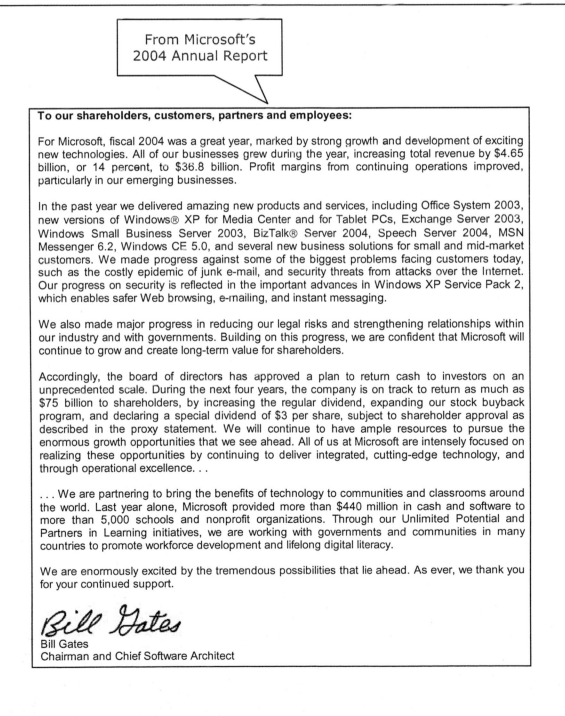

From Microsoft's 2004 Annual Report

To our shareholders, customers, partners and employees:

For Microsoft, fiscal 2004 was a great year, marked by strong growth and development of exciting new technologies. All of our businesses grew during the year, increasing total revenue by $4.65 billion, or 14 percent, to $36.8 billion. Profit margins from continuing operations improved, particularly in our emerging businesses.

In the past year we delivered amazing new products and services, including Office System 2003, new versions of Windows® XP for Media Center and for Tablet PCs, Exchange Server 2003, Windows Small Business Server 2003, BizTalk® Server 2004, Speech Server 2004, MSN Messenger 6.2, Windows CE 5.0, and several new business solutions for small and mid-market customers. We made progress against some of the biggest problems facing customers today, such as the costly epidemic of junk e-mail, and security threats from attacks over the Internet. Our progress on security is reflected in the important advances in Windows XP Service Pack 2, which enables safer Web browsing, e-mailing, and instant messaging.

We also made major progress in reducing our legal risks and strengthening relationships within our industry and with governments. Building on this progress, we are confident that Microsoft will continue to grow and create long-term value for shareholders.

Accordingly, the board of directors has approved a plan to return cash to investors on an unprecedented scale. During the next four years, the company is on track to return as much as $75 billion to shareholders, by increasing the regular dividend, expanding our stock buyback program, and declaring a special dividend of $3 per share, subject to shareholder approval as described in the proxy statement. We will continue to have ample resources to pursue the enormous growth opportunities that we see ahead. All of us at Microsoft are intensely focused on realizing these opportunities by continuing to deliver integrated, cutting-edge technology, and through operational excellence. . .

. . . We are partnering to bring the benefits of technology to communities and classrooms around the world. Last year alone, Microsoft provided more than $440 million in cash and software to more than 5,000 schools and nonprofit organizations. Through our Unlimited Potential and Partners in Learning initiatives, we are working with governments and communities in many countries to promote workforce development and lifelong digital literacy.

We are enormously excited by the tremendous possibilities that lie ahead. As ever, we thank you for your continued support.

Bill Gates

Bill Gates
Chairman and Chief Software Architect

FINANCIAL HIGHLIGHTS

➜ Key financial statistics for a company's most recent 5-10 fiscal year period.

Figure 6. Financial highlights

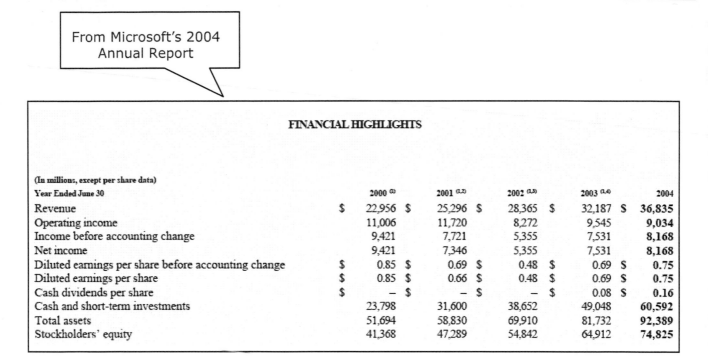

From Microsoft's 2004 Annual Report

FINANCIAL HIGHLIGHTS

(In millions, except per share data)

Year Ended June 30		2000 [3]		2001 [1,2]		2002 [1,3]		2003 [1,4]		2004
Revenue	$	22,956	$	25,296	$	28,365	$	32,187	$	36,835
Operating income		11,006		11,720		8,272		9,545		9,034
Income before accounting change		9,421		7,721		5,355		7,531		8,168
Net income		9,421		7,346		5,355		7,531		8,168
Diluted earnings per share before accounting change	$	0.85	$	0.69	$	0.48	$	0.69	$	0.75
Diluted earnings per share	$	0.85	$	0.66	$	0.48	$	0.69	$	0.75
Cash dividends per share	$	–	$	–	$	–	$	0.08	$	0.16
Cash and short-term investments		23,798		31,600		38,652		49,048		60,592
Total assets		51,694		58,830		69,910		81,732		92,389
Stockholders' equity		41,368		47,289		54,842		64,912		74,825

MANAGEMENT'S DISCUSSION AND ANALYSIS

➔ Management's Discussion and Analysis (MD&A) is a treasure trove of information. It usually includes:

1. An overview of the company's operations (often segment by segment)
2. Selected financial data for the completed year
3. Projections and expectations for the following year(s)
4. Important accounting policy changes

➔ The MD&A section spans a number of pages and provides detailed information that should be reviewed carefully.

Figure 7. Management's discussion & analysis

From Wal-Mart's 2004 Annual Report

Management's Discussion and Analysis of Results of Operations and Financial Condition

We intend for this discussion to provide the reader with information that will assist in understanding our financial statements, the changes in certain key items in those financial statements from year to year, and the primary factors that accounted for those changes, as well as how certain accounting principles affect our financial statements. The discussion also provides information about the financial results of the various segments of our business to provide a better understanding of how those segments and their results affect the financial condition and results of operations of the Company as a whole. This discussion should be read in conjunction with our financial statements as of January 31, 2004, and the year then ended and the notes accompanying those financial statements.

Overview

Wal-Mart is a global retailer committed to growing by improving the standard of living for our Customers throughout the world. We earn the trust of our Customers every day by providing a broad assortment of quality merchandise and services at every day low prices ("EDLP") while fostering a culture that rewards and embraces mutual respect, integrity and diversity. EDLP is our pricing philosophy under which we price items at a low price every day so that our Customers trust that our prices will not change erratically under frequent promotional activity. SAM'S CLUB is in business for small businesses. Our focus for SAM'S CLUB is to provide exceptional value on brand-name merchandise at "member's only" prices for both business and personal use. Internationally, we operate with similar philosophies.

FINANCIAL STATEMENTS

➔ Financial statements, along with the accompanying footnotes, represent the heart of an Annual Report as well as 10-K and 10-Q. They allow readers to analyze a company's financial performance and health:

1. Consolidated Income Statement
2. Consolidated Balance Sheet
3. Consolidated Statement of Cash Flows
4. Consolidated Statements of Stockholders' Equity

➔ For the purposes of financial analysis, the three core financial statements are #1-3 above.

What does "consolidated" mean?

Consolidated simply means that these financial reports contain financial information of all businesses majority-owned by a parent company.

In the case of Berkshire Hathaway, which owns 40 companies (including Fruit of the Loom®, Benjamin Moore, and International Dairy Queen) and is run by Warren Buffett, the company reports its financial results as a consolidated entity, encompassing all of its majority-owned businesses.

THE INCOME STATEMENT

➜ Represents a company's operating performance over a specific period of time through a summary of the company's revenues and expenses, showing net earnings (profit) or loss.

Also referred to as:

⟳ The Consolidated Statement of Earnings

⟳ The Profit and Loss (P&L) Statement

⟳ Statement of Revenues and Expenses

Figure 8. The income statement

CVS' 2004 Consolidated Income Statement

	Fiscal Year Ended		
In millions, except per share amounts	Jan. 1, 2005 (52 weeks)	Jan. 3, 2004 (53 weeks)	Dec. 28, 2002 (52 weeks)
Net sales	$30,594.3	$26,588.0	$24,181.5
Cost of goods sold, buying and warehousing costs	22,563.1	19,725.0	18,112.7
Gross margin	8,031.2	6,863.0	6,068.8
Selling, general and administrative expenses	6,079.7	5,097.7	4,552.3
Depreciation and amortization	496.8	341.7	310.3
Total operating expenses	6,576.5	5,439.4	4,862.6
Operating profit	1,454.7	1,423.6	1,206.2
Interest expense, net	58.3	48.1	50.4
Earnings before income tax provision	1,396.4	1,375.5	1,155.8
Income tax provision	477.6	528.2	439.2
Net earnings	918.8	847.3	716.6
Preference dividends, net of income tax benefit	14.2	14.6	14.8
Net earnings available to common shareholders	$ 904.6	$ 832.7	$ 701.8
Basic earnings per common share:			
Net earnings	$ 2.27	$ 2.11	$ 1.79
Weighted average common shares outstanding	398.6	394.4	392.3
Diluted earnings per common share:			
Net earnings	$ 2.20	$ 2.06	$ 1.75
Weighted average common shares outstanding	415.4	407.7	405.3
Dividends declared per common share	$ 0.265	$ 0.230	$ 0.230

THE BALANCE SHEET

→ Shows a company's resources (assets) and how those resources were funded (liabilities and shareholders' equity) on a particular date (end of the quarter, end of the year).[1]

Also referred to as:

⊃ Statement of Financial Position

Figure 9. The balance sheet

On January 1, 2005

On January 1, 2004

CVS' 2004 Consolidated Balance Sheet

In millions, except shares and per share amounts	Jan. 1, 2005	Jan. 3, 2004
Assets:		
Cash and cash equivalents	$ 392.3	$ 843.2
Accounts receivable, net	1,764.2	1,349.6
Inventories	5,453.9	4,016.5
Deferred income taxes	243.1	252.1
Other current assets	66.0	35.1
Total current assets	7,919.5	6,496.5
Property and equipment, net	3,505.9	2,542.1
Goodwill	1,898.6	889.0
Intangible assets, net	867.9	403.7
Deferred income taxes	137.6	—
Other assets	217.4	211.8
Total assets	$14,546.8	$10,543.1
Liabilities:		
Accounts payable	$ 2,275.9	$ 1,666.4
Accrued expenses	1,666.7	1,499.6
Short-term debt	885.6	—
Current portion of long-term debt	30.6	323.2
Total current liabilities	4,858.8	3,489.2
Long-term debt	1,925.9	753.1
Deferred income taxes	—	41.6
Other long-term liabilities	774.9	237.4
Commitments and contingencies (Note 9)		
Shareholders' equity:		
Preferred stock, $0.01 par value: authorized 120,619 shares; no shares issued or outstanding	—	—
Preference stock, series one ESOP convertible, par value $1.00: authorized 50,000,000 shares; issued and outstanding 4,273,000 shares at January 1, 2005 and 4,541,000 shares at January 3, 2004	228.4	242.7
Common stock, par value $0.01: authorized 1,000,000,000 shares; issued 414,276,000 shares at January 1, 2005 and 410,187,000 shares at January 3, 2004	4.2	4.1
Treasury stock, at cost: 13,317,000 shares at January 1, 2005 and 14,803,000 shares at January 3, 2004	(385.9)	(428.6)
Guaranteed ESOP obligation	(140.9)	(163.2)
Capital surplus	1,691.4	1,557.2
Retained earnings	5,645.5	4,846.5
Accumulated other comprehensive loss	(55.5)	(36.9)
Total shareholders' equity	6,987.2	6,021.8
Total liabilities and shareholders' equity	$14,546.8	$10,543.1

[1] To be discussed in detail in Chapter 6

THE CASH FLOW STATEMENT

➔ The cash flow statement is a summary of the cash inflows and outflows of a business over a specified period of time (quarter or year).

Figure 10. The cash flow statement

CVS' 2004 Cash Flow Statement

	Fiscal Year Ended		
In millions	Jan. 1, 2005 (52 weeks)	Jan. 3, 2004 (53 weeks)	Dec. 28, 2002 (52 weeks)
Cash flows from operating activities:			
Cash receipts from sales	$ 30,545.8	$ 26,276.9	$ 24,128.4
Cash paid for inventory	(22,469.2)	(19,262.9)	(17,715.1)
Cash paid to other suppliers and employees	(6,528.5)	(5,475.5)	(4,832.5)
Interest and dividends received	5.7	5.7	4.1
Interest paid	(70.4)	(64.9)	(60.6)
Income taxes paid	(569.2)	(510.4)	(319.5)
Net cash provided by operating activities	914.2	968.9	1,204.8
Cash flows from investing activities:			
Additions to property and equipment	(1,347.7)	(1,121.7)	(1,108.8)
Proceeds from sale-leaseback transactions	496.6	487.8	448.8
Acquisitions, net of cash and investments	(2,293.7)	(133.1)	(93.5)
Cash outflow from hedging activities	(32.8)	—	—
Proceeds from sale or disposal of assets	14.3	13.4	17.7
Net cash used in investing activities	(3,163.3)	(753.6)	(735.8)
Cash flows from financing activities:			
Reductions in long-term debt	(301.5)	(0.8)	(3.1)
Additions to long-term debt	1,204.1	—	300.0
Proceeds from exercise of stock options	129.8	38.3	34.0
Dividends paid	(119.8)	(105.2)	(104.9)
Purchase of treasury shares	—	—	—
Additions to/ (reductions in) short-term debt	885.6	(4.8)	(230.9)
Net cash provided by (used in) financing activities	1,798.2	(72.5)	(4.9)
Net (decrease) increase in cash and cash equivalents	(450.9)	142.8	464.1
Cash and cash equivalents at beginning of year	843.2	700.4	236.3
Cash and cash equivalents at end of year	$ 392.3	$ 843.2	$ 700.4

NOTES TO CONSOLIDATED STATEMENTS

➔ Notes to Consolidated Statements provide supplementary information to consolidated financial statements and are considered an integral part of the financial report (they must be read as thoroughly as the financial statements themselves!) They can be separated into three major categories:

1. SUMMARY OF ACCOUNTING POLICIES

➔ Summary of Significant Accounting Policies provides an overview of major GAAP used by a company in the preparation of its financial statements.

2. EXPLANATORY NOTES

➔ Explanatory Notes offer a detailed overview on a number of supplementary financial metrics, including:

  ⇨ Fixed assets
  ⇨ Stock options
  ⇨ Financing and debt
  ⇨ Leases
  ⇨ Shareholders' equity
  ⇨ Taxes
  ⇨ Employee benefit plans

McDonald's 2004 Annual Report

Notes to consolidated financial statements

Summary of significant accounting policies

Nature of business
The Company primarily operates and franchises McDonald's restaurants in the food service industry. The Company also operates Boston Market and Chipotle Mexican Grill in the U.S. and has a minority ownership in U.K.-based Pret A Manger. In December 2003, the Company sold its Donatos Pizzeria business.

All restaurants are operated either by the Company, by independent entrepreneurs under the terms of franchise arrangements (franchisees), or by affiliates operating under license agreements.

Consolidation
The consolidated financial statements include the accounts of the Company and its subsidiaries. Substantially all investments in affiliates owned 50% or less (primarily McDonald's Japan) are accounted for by the equity method.

Estimates in financial statements
The preparation of financial statements in conformity with accounting principles generally accepted in the U.S. requires management to make estimates and assumptions that affect the amounts reported in the financial statements and accompanying notes. Actual results could differ from those estimates.

3. SUPPLEMENTARY INFORMATION NOTES

➔ Supplementary Information Notes provide additional details about a company's operations, including:

  ⇨ A listing of reserves for an oil & gas company
  ⇨ Breakdown of unit sales by product line

REPORT OF MANAGEMENT'S RESPONSIBILITIES

➔ Three responsibilities of management include:

1. Preparing the company's financial statements and reports.

2. Being responsible for the company's internal financial controls.

3. Allowing company directors and independent auditors to carry out their respective roles in assuring the accuracy of the company's financial statements.

Figure 11. Report of management's responsibilities

McDonald's 2004 Annual Report

Management's Report

Management is responsible for the preparation, integrity and fair presentation of the consolidated financial statements and Notes to the consolidated financial statements. The financial statements were prepared in accordance with the accounting principles generally accepted in the U.S. and include certain amounts based on management's judgement and best estimates. Other financial information presented is consistent with the financial statements.

Management is also responsible for establishing and maintaining adequate internal control over financial reporting as defined in Rules 13a-15(f) and 15d-15(f) under the Securities Exchange Act of 1934. The Company's internal control over financial reporting is designed under the supervision of the Company's principal executive and financial officers in order to provide reasonable assurance regarding the reliability of financial reporting and the preparation of financial statements for external purposes in accordance with generally accepted accounting principles. The Company's internal control over financial reporting includes those policies and procedures that:

(i) Pertain to the maintenance of records that, in reasonable detail, accurately and fairly reflect the transactions and dispositions of assets of the Company;

(ii) Provide reasonable assurance that transactions are recorded as necessary to permit preparation of financial statements in accordance with generally accepted accounting principles, and that receipts and expenditures of the Company are being made only in accordance with authorizations of management and directors of the Company; and

(iii) Provide reasonable assurance regarding prevention or timely detection of unauthorized acquisition, use or disposition of the Company's assets that could have a material effect on the financial statements.

Because of its inherent limitations, internal control over financial reporting may not prevent or detect misstatements. Also, projections of any evaluation of effectiveness to future periods are subject to the risk that controls may become inadequate because of changes in conditions, or that the degree of compliance with the policies or procedures may deteriorate.

Management assessed the effectiveness of the Company's internal control over financial reporting as of December 31, 2004. In making this assessment, management used the criteria established in Internal Control-Integrated Framework issued by the Committee of Sponsoring Organizations of the Treadway Commission (COSO).

Based on our assessment and those criteria, management believes that the Company maintained effective internal control over financial reporting as of December 31, 2004.

The Company's independent registered public accounting firm, Ernst & Young LLP, has issued an attestation report on management's assessment of the Company's internal control over financial reporting. That report appears on page 46 of this Report and expresses unqualified opinions on management's assessment and on the effectiveness of the Company's internal control over financial reporting.

McDonald's Corporation
February 22, 2005

RISK FACTORS

➔ This section consists of legal boilerplate material spanning a number of pages and covering both industry- and company-specific risks.

➔ A close look at this section could yield important red flags while allowing the readers to familiarize themselves with some of the industry dynamics in which that company operates.

Figure 12. Risk factors

Microsoft 2004 Annual Report

ISSUES AND UNCERTAINTIES

This Annual Report contains statements that are forward-looking. These statements are based on current expectations and assumptions that are subject to risks and uncertainties. Actual results could differ materially because of issues and uncertainties such as those listed below and elsewhere in this report, which, among others, should be considered in evaluating our future financial performance.

Challenges to our Business Model. Since our inception, our business model has been based upon customers agreeing to pay a fee to license software developed and distributed by us. Under this commercial software model, software developers bear the costs of converting original ideas into software products through investments in research and development, offsetting these costs with the revenue received from the distribution of their products. We believe the commercial software model has had substantial benefits for users of software, allowing them to rely on our expertise and the expertise of other software developers that have powerful incentives to develop innovative software that is useful, reliable, and compatible with other software and hardware. In recent years, there has been a growing challenge to the commercial software model. Under the non-commercial software model, open source software produced by loosely associated groups of unpaid programmers and made available for license to end users without charge is distributed by firms at nominal cost that earn revenue on complementary services and products, without having to bear the full costs of research and development for the open source software. The most notable example of open source software is the Linux operating system. While we believe our products provide customers with significant advantages in security and productivity, and generally have a lower total cost of ownership than open source software, the popularization of the non-commercial software model continues to pose a significant challenge to our business model, including recent efforts by proponents of open source software to convince governments worldwide to mandate the use of open source software in their purchase and deployment of software products. To the extent open source software gains increasing market acceptance, sales of our products may decline, we may have to reduce the prices we charge for our products, and revenue and operating margins may consequently decline.

LEGAL PROCEEDINGS

→ This section highlights key legal proceedings (i.e. lawsuits) facing the company.

→ It is important to note that almost every corporation typically faces a number of lawsuits, so you should not be alarmed to find this section in an annual report (as well as in a 10-K filing).

→ Take a close look at these legal proceedings – they may yield important information, such as monetary damages being sought against the company.

Figure 13. Legal proceedings

Microsoft 2004 Annual Report

Litigation. As discussed in Note 17 – Contingencies of the Notes to Financial Statements, we are subject to a variety of claims and lawsuits. Adverse outcomes in some or all of the pending cases may result in significant monetary damages or injunctive relief against us. We are also subject to a variety of other claims and suits that arise from time to time in the ordinary course of our business. While management currently believes that resolving all of these matters, individually or in the aggregate, will not have a material adverse impact on our financial position or results of operations, the litigation and other claims noted above are subject to inherent uncertainties and management's view of these matters may change in the future. There exists the possibility of a material adverse impact on our financial position and the results of operations for the period in which the effect of an unfavorable final outcome becomes probable and reasonably estimable.

REPORT OF INDEPENDENT AUDITORS

➔ Financial information contained in annual reports is independently verified by Certified Public Accountants (CPA), whose summary report is presented in the *Report of Independent Auditors* section of an annual report.

REPORT OF INDEPENDENT AUDITORS

➜ Typically consists of three paragraphs:

⇨ **Paragraph 1:** Indicates that this annual report has been audited, and distinguishes between the respective responsibilities of the company management (to prepare these financial reports) and the auditing firm (to audit them).

⇨ **Paragraph 2:** (scope section) indicates that auditors' examination was performed in accordance with GAAP.

⇨ **Paragraph 3:** (opinion section) describes the results of auditors' examination i.e. auditors' opinion that financial statements have been prepared in accordance with GAAP.

⇨ **Paragraph 4:** may or may not appear, discussing any accounting methods that have not been consistent across different periods.

Figure 14. Report of independent auditors

McDonald's 2004 Annual Report

Report of Independent Registered Public Accounting Firm

The Board of Directors and Shareholders
McDonald's Corporation

We have audited the accompanying Consolidated balance sheets of McDonald's Corporation as of December 31, 2004 and 2003, and the related Consolidated statements of income, shareholders' equity and cash flows for each of the three years in the period ended December 31, 2004. These financial statements are the responsibility of McDonald's Corporation management. Our responsibility is to express an opinion on these financial statements based on our audits.

We conducted our audits in accordance with the standards of the Public Company Accounting Oversight Board (United States). Those standards require that we plan and perform the audit to obtain reasonable assurance about whether the financial statements are free of material misstatement. An audit includes examining, on a test basis, evidence supporting the amounts and disclosures in the financial statements. An audit also includes assessing the accounting principles used and significant estimates made by management, as well as evaluating the overall financial statement presentation. We believe that our audits provide a reasonable basis for our opinion.

In our opinion, the financial statements referred to above present fairly, in all material respects, the consolidated financial position of McDonald's Corporation at December 31, 2004 and 2003, and the consolidated results of its operations and its cash flows for each of the three years in the period ended December 31, 2004, in conformity with U.S. generally accepted accounting principles.

As discussed in the Notes to the consolidated financial statements, effective January 1, 2003, the Company changed its method for accounting for asset retirement obligations to conform with SFAS No.143, *Accounting for Asset Retirement Obligations.* Effective January 1, 2002, the Company changed its method for accounting for goodwill to conform with SFAS No.142, *Goodwill and Other Intangible Assets.*

We also have audited, in accordance with the standards of the Public Company Accounting Oversight Board (United States), the effectiveness of McDonald's Corporation's internal control over financial reporting as of December 31, 2004, based on criteria established in Internal Control–Integrated Framework issued by the Committee of Sponsoring Organizations of the Treadway Commission and our report dated February 22, 2005 expressed an unqualified opinion thereon.

Ernst & Young LLP
Chicago, Illinois
February 22, 2005

DIRECTORS & OFFICERS

➔ This section lists executive officers of a company as well as its Directors (i.e. Members of the Board) and their past and current professional affiliations

Figure 15. Directors & officers

Microsoft 2004 Annual Report

DIRECTORS AND EXECUTIVE OFFICERS OF MICROSOFT CORPORATION

DIRECTORS

William H. Gates III
Chairman,
Chief Software Architect,
Microsoft Corporation

Steven A. Ballmer
Chief Executive Officer,
Microsoft Corporation

James I. Cash Jr., PhD. [1,5]
Former James E. Robison
Professor,
Harvard Business School

Raymond V. Gilmartin [4,5]
Chairman, President,
Chief Executive Officer,
Merck & Co., Inc.

Ann McLaughlin Korologos [2,5]
Chairman Emeritus,
The Aspen Institute;
Senior Advisor,
Benedetto, Gartland & Co., Inc.

David F. Marquardt [3,4]
General Partner,
August Capital

Charles H. Noski [1,3]
Corporate Vice President,
Chief Financial Officer,
Northrop Grumman Corporation

Helmut Panke [2]
Chairman of the Board of
Management, BMW AG

Wm. G. Reed Jr. [*,1,2]
Former Chairman,
Simpson Investment Company

Jon A. Shirley [3]
Former President,
Chief Operating Officer,
Microsoft Corporation

Board Committees
1. Audit Committee
2. Compensation Committee
3. Finance Committee
4. Governance and Nominating Committee
5. Antitrust Compliance Committee
* Retiring in November 2004

EXECUTIVE OFFICERS

William H. Gates III
Chairman of the Board;
Chief Software Architect

Steven A. Ballmer
Chief Executive Officer

James E. Allchin
Group Vice President,
Platforms Group

Robert J. (Robbie) Bach
Senior Vice President,
Home and Entertainment

Douglas J. Burgum
Senior Vice President,
Microsoft Business Solutions

David W. Cole
Senior Vice President, MSN
and Personal Services Group

John G. Connors
Senior Vice President;
Chief Financial Officer

Jean-Philippe Courtois
Senior Vice President;
CEO, Microsoft Europe,
Middle East, and Africa

Kenneth A. DiPietro
Corporate Vice President,
Human Resources

Kevin R. Johnson
Group Vice President,
Worldwide Sales,
Marketing and Services

Michelle (Mich) Mathews
Corporate Vice President,
Marketing

Craig J. Mundie
Senior Vice President;
Chief Technical Officer,
Advanced Strategies
and Policy

Jeffrey S. Raikes
Group Vice President,
Information Worker Business

Eric D. Rudder
Senior Vice President,
Server and Tools Business

Bradford L. Smith
Senior Vice President,
General Counsel and Secretary

David Vaskevitch
Senior Vice President;
Chief Technical Officer,
Business Platforms

SUMMARY

Letter to Stockholders	A marketing piece summarizing a company's recent achievements and near-term strategic initiatives
Financial Highlights	Key financial statistics for a company's most recent 5-10 fiscal year period
Financial Statements	Consolidated Statement of Earnings (Income Statement) Consolidated Balance Sheet Consolidated Statement of Cash Flows Consolidated Statements of Stockholders' Equity
Notes to Consolidated Statements	Provide supplementary information to consolidated financial statements Summary of significant accounting policies a company uses in preparation of its financial statements
Report of Management's Responsibilities	Overview of management's responsibilities relating to financial statement preparation
Management's Discussion and Analysis	Summary and analysis of the company's financial results for the completed year
Risk Factors	Summary of industry- and company-specific risks
Legal Proceedings	Overview of key legal proceedings against a company
Report of Independent Auditors	Summary opinion of an independent auditor relating to financial statements and their preparation
Directors & Officers	Summary of top company executives and Directors

SUMMARY

➔ **ON-LINE EXERCISE**

⇨ Please log on to
www.wallstreetprep.com/accounting.html

⇨ Download and save the Word file titled: "Reading
the Annual Report"

⇨ Complete the exercise

CHAPTER 5

INCOME STATEMENT

INCOME STATEMENT

WHAT IS THE INCOME STATEMENT?

→ The income statement is a financial report that depicts the operating performance of a company (i.e. revenues less expenses generated – i.e. profitability) over a specific period of time (typically a quarter or year).

WHY IS IT IMPORTANT?

→ It facilitates the analysis of a company's growth prospects, cost structure, and profitability.

→ Analysts can use the income statement to identify the components and sources ("drivers") of net earnings.

Also referred to as:

⊃ The Consolidated Statement of Earnings

⊃ The Profit and Loss (P&L) Statement

⊃ Statement of Revenues and Expenses

MAJOR TYPICAL COMPONENTS & THEIR DEFINITIONS

Net Revenues	Total dollar payment for goods and services that are credited to an income statement over a particular time period.
Cost of Goods Sold	Cost of Goods sold represents a company's direct cost of manufacture (for manufacturers) or procurement (for merchandisers) of a good or service that the company sells to generate revenue.
Gross Profit	Revenues - Cost of Goods Sold
Selling, General & Administrative (SG&A)	Operating costs not directly associated with the production or procurement of the product or service that the company sells to generate revenue. Payroll, wages, commissions, meal and travel expenses, stationary, advertising, and marketing expenses fall under this line item.
Research & Development (R&D)	A company's activities that are directed at developing new products or procedures.
Earnings Before Interest, Taxes, Depreciation & Amortization (EBITDA)	Gross Profit - SG&A - R&D. EBITDA is a popular measure of a company's financial performance.
Depreciation & Amortization (D&A)	The allocation of cost over a fixed asset's useful life in order to match the timing of the cost of the asset with when it is expected to generate revenue benefits.
Other Operating Expenses / Income	Any operating expenses not allocated to COGS, SG&A, R&D, D&A
Earnings Before Interest & Taxes (EBIT)	EBITDA - D&A
Interest Expense	Interest expense is the amount the company has to pay on debt owed. This could be to bondholders or to banks. Interest expense subtracted from EBIT equals earnings before taxes (EBT).
Interest Income	A company's income from its cash holdings and investments (stocks, bonds, and savings accounts).
Unusual or Infrequent Income / Expenses	Gain (loss) on sale of assets, disposal of a business segment, impairment charge, write-offs, restructuring costs.
Income Tax Expense	The tax liability a company reports on the income statement.
Net Income	EBIT - Net Interest Expense - Other Nonoperating Income - Taxes
Basic Earnings per Share (EPS)	Net income / Basic Weighted Average Shares Outstanding
Diluted EPS	Net income / Diluted Weighted Average Shares Outstanding

INCOME STATEMENT

REVENUES

Definition

➔ Revenues represent proceeds from the sale of goods and services produced or offered by a company.

> ➲ You will see revenues represented on the income statement as Revenues, Sales, Net Sales or Net Revenues. We'll explain what is being "netted" out of net revenues shortly.
>
> ➲ Revenues are referred to colloquially as a company's top-line.

Not all income is revenue

A company may have other income streams, which are not related to its main operations:

⇨ Interest income earned from investments

⇨ Income received from a legal settlement

⇨ These are not recorded as revenues, but rather as *Other Income*, and accounted for on the income statement in a line item below Revenues.

> **Examples of revenues include:**
>
> ➲ Sale of crude oil by ExxonMobil
>
> ➲ Sale of books by Amazon.com
>
> ➲ Sale of hamburgers by McDonald's

REVENUES

Exercise: CVS

In February 2005, CVS, a drugstore chain, recorded the following transactions:

❑ Sold $500m in merchandise

❑ Sold $100m in prescriptions

❑ Won a legal settlement of $400m

❑ Collected $20m in interest income from a bank account

Record total revenues for CVS in February 2005

INCOME STATEMENT

REVENUES

Solution: CVS

☑ Sold $500m in merchandise

☑ Sold $100m in prescriptions

☐ Won a legal settlement of $400m

☐ Collected $20m in interest income from a bank account

Total revenue = $600m (merchandise and prescriptions)

⇨ Legal settlement and interest income are NOT part of revenues (Non-operating income)

REVENUES

Bad Debt Expense

➜ Recall that we mentioned that revenues are presented as Net Sales or Net Revenues on the income statement.

➜ This is because bad debt expense is being netted against gross revenues, and the income statement simply represents the consolidated line item as revenues, net of bad debt expense.

What is bad debt expense?

➜ When companies sell their products, some customers may ultimately not pay. Companies are therefore required to estimate this uncollectible amount (referred to as Bad Debt Expense) at the time of sale.

➜ Net revenues include the financial impact of returned goods and uncollectible payment (Bad Debt) from customers.

➜ Net Revenues = Gross Revenues – Bad Debt Expense

In the real world

Microsoft recorded net revenues of $36,800 million in 2004. Per the company's footnotes, we discover:

Gross sales = $36,844m

Bad debt expense = $36,844m - $36,800m = $44m

INCOME STATEMENT

REVENUES

Revenue Recognition: To Recognize and When?

➔ Recall that accrual basis of accounting dictates that revenues must be recorded only when they are earned <u>and</u> measurable.

➔ Recall the Amazon.com exercise: Amazon.com received a $20 book order on 12/29/04, but it could only record it as revenue once it was shipped on 1/4/05.

➔ According to the revenue recognition principle, a company cannot record revenue until it is earned – that is, until that order is shipped to a customer <u>and</u> collection from that customer, who used a credit card, is reasonably assured.

➔ Deciding when to recognize revenues can be less straight-forward for some companies than for Amazon.com. For instance, how should companies engaged in long-term projects recognize revenue?

Revenue Recognition: Long-term projects

➔ For long-term projects, companies have some flexibility with respect to revenue recognition:

1. **Percentage of Completion method**
   ⇨ Revenues are recognized on the basis of the percentage of total work completed during the accounting period.

2. **Completed Contract method**
   ⇨ Rarely used in the U.S., this method allows revenue recognition only once the entire project has been completed.

INCOME STATEMENT

REVENUES

Exercise: Boeing

On January 12, 2005, Boeing agreed to deliver 6 Boeing airplanes to Bavaria Aircraft Leasing for $330 million. Delivery of the airplanes begins in 2005 and extends through 2007. Boeing is paid upon delivery of each plane.

Assuming Boeing uses the percentage of completion method, when should Boeing recognize $330 million of revenues?

- ❏ On January 12, 2005 – announcement date of this contract

- ❏ Sometime during the 2005-2007 period – as it delivers each of these planes to the customer

- ❏ At the end of 2007 – when all of the planes have been delivered

- ❏ In 2008 – when all six airplanes are in service

REVENUES

Solution: Boeing

□   On January 12, 2005 – announcement date of this contract

☑   Sometime during the 2005-2007 period – as it delivers each of these planes to the customer

□   At the end of 2007 – when all of the planes have been delivered

□   In 2008 – when all six airplanes are in service

INCOME STATEMENT

REVENUES

Expense Recognition & Accrual Basis of Accounting

→ When should Boeing record costs associated with producing those six airplanes?

The Matching Principle

→ The Matching Principle states that expenses should be "matched" to revenues. In other words, the costs of manufacturing a product are matched to the revenue generated from that product during the same period.

Matching principle in action
⮑ Costs associated with the production of the book by Amazon.com must be recorded in the same period as the revenue from its sale.
⮑ Costs associated with the production of airplanes by Boeing must be recorded in the same period as the revenue from their sale.

Putting It All Together – The Accrual Basis of Accounting

→ Revenues and expenses are recognized and recorded when *an economic exchange occurs,* not necessarily when cash is exchanged.

→ This is the core principle of the accrual basis of accounting, which measures a company's performance by recognizing economic events regardless of when cash transactions happen.

Why use accrual accounting?

→ Accrual accounting presents a more accurate depiction of a company's operations.

→ In the case of Boeing, its recognition of $330 million of revenues will likely take place in regular intervals, in step with the completion of airplane production and delivery.

→ Accrual accounting attempts to present a more accurate depiction of a company's operating performance by matching costs with revenues.

→ For the purposes of financial analysis, the matching principle facilitates making projections of future results.

What if the accrual concept were not used?

⮑ In the Boeing example, Boeing presumably had to purchase raw materials (metal, plane parts, etc.) some time ago, before *any* revenues from its contract with Bavaria Leasing were recognized.

⮑ If it did not match revenues with expenses, it would have reported the material costs back when they were acquired on their financial statements. The financials would show a company with high costs and no revenues.

⮑ This, of course, would not be an accurate depiction of the company's profitability because we know that Boeing bought those raw materials for the purpose of fulfilling an order which will generate future revenues.

⮑ By matching costs with revenues, the accrual concept strives to more accurately depict a company's operating results.

Accrual Versus Cash Accounting – What's the Difference?

→ Although the benefits of the accrual method should by now be apparent, it does by definition have the limitation that analysts cannot track objectively the movement of cash.

→ Cash accounting *objectively* recognizes revenues when cash is received and records costs when cash is paid out; accrual accounting involves *subjectivity* in regards to the allocation of revenues and expenses to different periods.

→ Public companies are required to use accrual accounting in accordance with GAAP. Cash accounting may be used by small businesses (a coffee shop) and is used by U.S. federal government in its budget reporting.

→ The cash flow statement, one of the three principal financial statements, allows analysts to reconcile these differences.

	Cash Accounting	Accrual Accounting
Purpose	Track movement of cash	Allocate revenues and expenses to create a more accurate depiction of operations
Revenue Recognition	Cash is received	Economic exchange is almost or fully complete
Expense Recognition	Cash is paid out – could be in a different period from revenue recognition	Expenses associated with a product must be recorded during the same period as revenue generated from it (Matching Principle)
Judgment	Movement of cash is *objective*	Allocation of revenues and expenses to different periods is *subjective*
Key Takeaway	Under accrual accounting, some revenues and expenses are reported in periods that are different from those in which cash was actually received or spent!	

REVENUES

Revenue manipulation

→ Revenue recognition cannot be performed completely accurately, and under U.S. GAAP, company management must therefore utilize conservative estimates and judgments.

→ However, companies' flexibility in revenue recognition creates potential for manipulation in the form of increased revenue through the use of improper techniques.

→ Revenue recognition methods are almost always explained in the Notes to Consolidated Statements and must be read carefully!

In the real world – TSAI in 1998

⊃ Software maker TSAI sold 5-year license agreements for its software.

⊃ In accordance with conservative revenue recognition rules, the company only recorded revenues from these agreements when the customers were billed through the course of the 5-year agreement.

⊃ The company began experiencing slowing sales in 1998. To hide the problem, it changed its revenue recognition practices to record nearly 5 years' worth of revenues upfront, thereby artificially boosting sales.

⊃ The gimmick caught up to the company a year later when investors compared 1999 results to 1998 results and saw a 20% decline in revenues.

INCOME STATEMENT

COST OF GOODS SOLD

Definition

→ Cost of Goods Sold, often referred to as COGS or CGS, represents a company's direct cost of manufacture (for manufacturers) or procurement (for merchandisers) of a good or service that the company sells to generate revenue.

Examples of COGS
- Raw material costs
- Direct factory labor
- Delivery costs
- Any other costs directly associated with the generation of revenue

COGS do not include administrative costs

→ Costs such as administrative and marketing expenses which cannot be directly attributed to the manufacture of products are not included in COGS.

→ Those costs are included under Selling, General & Administrative Expenses (discussed in the following section).

COST OF GOODS SOLD

Exercise: COGS

Which of the following examples constitute Cost of Goods Sold?

❑ Cost of steel for auto manufacturer

❑ Cost of a cashier at a supermarket

❑ Cost of computers used by secretaries at a tire plant

❑ Cost of computers acquired by merchant for resale to the public

❑ Cost of research and development at a pharmaceutical company

COST OF GOODS SOLD

Solution: COGS

Which of the following examples constitute Cost of Goods Sold?

☑   Cost of steel for auto manufacturer

☐   Cost of a cashier at a supermarket

☐   Cost of computers used by secretaries at a tire plant

☑   Cost of computers acquired by merchant for resale to the public

☐   Cost of research and development at a pharmaceutical company

INCOME STATEMENT

GROSS PROFIT

➔ Gross profit represents profit after only direct expenses (COGS) have been accounted for:

> **Gross Profit = Net Revenues – COGS**

Exercise: Calculating gross profit

⇨ Tire manufacturer recorded $100m in net revenues

⇨ $40m in costs for rubber

⇨ $5m in shipping rubber to its plant

⇨ $20m in costs for office supplies

Calculate gross profit

INCOME STATEMENT

GROSS PROFIT

Solution: Calculating gross profit

Gross profit = Net Revenues – COGS = **$55m**

$20m in office supplies are not COGS

Gross profit margin (GPM)

Gross profit margin is expressed as a % and calculated as:

GPM = Gross Profit / Revenues

INCOME STATEMENT

SELLING, GENERAL & ADMINISTRATIVE

Definition

→ Selling, general, & administrative expenses, often abbreviated as SG&A or G&A, represent the operating expenses not directly associated with the production or procurement of the product or service that the company sells to generate revenue.

Examples of SG&A
⮑ Payroll
⮑ Wages
⮑ Commissions
⮑ Meal and travel expenses
⮑ Stationary, advertising, and marketing expenses

Exercise: SG&A

Which of the following constitute SG&A?

❑ Salaries of custodians at a tech company

❑ Office supplies

❑ Cost of computers used by staff at a consulting company

❑ Cost of maintenance of a factory machine

❑ Cost of business trip to Asia

SELLING, GENERAL & ADMINISTRATIVE

Exercise: SG&A

Which of the following constitute SG&A?

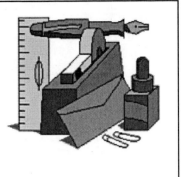

☑ Salaries of custodians at a tech company

☑ Office supplies

☑ Cost of computers used by staff at a consulting company

❏ Cost of maintenance of a factory machine

☑ Cost of business trip to Asia

RESEARCH & DEVELOPMENT (R&D)

Definition

➜ Research and development (R&D) expenses stem from a company's activities that are directed at developing new products or procedures.

➜ Research-intensive industries such as healthcare and technology often identify R&D expenses separately because they constitute such a large component of total expenses.

➜ For example, Microsoft, EMC, and Pfizer all identify R&D expenses separately.

➜ Other companies aggregate the R&D expense within Other Operating Expenses or SG&A.

INCOME STATEMENT

DEPRECIATION EXPENSE

Definition

→ Depreciation is a method by which the cost of long-term fixed assets (over 1 year) is spread over a future period (number of years), when these assets are expected to be in service and help generate revenue for a company.

→ Depreciation quantifies the wear and tear (from use and passage of time) of the physical asset through a systematic decrease (depreciation) of the assets' book (historical) value.

Fixed assets must have physical substance. They include:

- Plants

- Machinery

- Equipment

- Furniture

- Fixtures

- Leasehold improvements

- Land is a fixed asset but is NOT depreciated

Major asset classes and their typical useful lives	
Building and improvements	5-50 years
Fixtures and equipment	5-12 years
Transportation equipment	2-5 years
Internally developed software	3 years
Land	Not depreciated

DEPRECIATION EXPENSE

Exercise: Depreciation

Which of the following need to be depreciated?

☐   Warehouse

☐   Administrative wages

☐   Office furniture

☐   Power plant

☐   Land used to build a supermarket

DEPRECIATION EXPENSE

Solution: Depreciation

Which of the following need to be depreciated?

- ☑ Warehouse

- ☐ Administrative wages – part of SG&A, not an asset

- ☑ Office furniture

- ☑ Power plant

- ☐ Land used to build a supermarket – land is never depreciated

DEPRECIATION EXPENSE

➔ When a company purchases an asset (such as a manufacturing facility, an airplane, or a conveyer belt) which is expected to generate benefits over future periods, the cost of that asset is not simply recognized during the year it was acquired.

➔ Rather, the cost is spread over that particular asset's *useful life* in order to <u>match</u> the timing of the cost of the asset with its expected revenue generation.

➔ This is the application of the matching principal of accrual accounting: expenses (costs) are matched to the period when revenue is earned as a result of using the asset.

Depreciation is a "phantom" non-cash expense

➔ Depreciation is a non-cash, tax-deductible expense and can make up a significant portion of total expenses on a company's income statement.

> **Where to find depreciation**
>
> ⊃ Depreciation expense is represented on the income statement, either within a line item titled Depreciation and Amortization, or aggregated within another line item (typically Cost of Goods Sold).
>
> ⊃ If you do not see depreciation expense separately identified on the income statement, it does not mean that the company has no depreciation expense!
>
> ⊃ It just means you need to do more digging. You will find it in the Cash Flow Statement as well as in the footnotes to the financial statements.

➔ Depreciation expense is an allocation of the costs of an original purchase of fixed assets over the estimated useful lives of those fixed assets.

➔ If a company acquires fixed assets (several manufacturing facilities, for example) in 2003, it has to pay for their total cost during the same year; however, on its income statement, the expense associated with the purchase is recorded over the useful life of those assets in the form of depreciation expense, in line with the matching principle.

➔ The depreciation expense does not depict any actual cash outflow (payment).

DEPRECIATION EXPENSE

Calculating Depreciation Expense: Straight-Line Depreciation Method

➡ Under the straight-line depreciation method, the depreciable cost of an asset is spread evenly over the asset's estimated useful life.

➡ Accordingly, depreciation expense for each period (quarter or year) is the same, and can be calculated as follows:

$$\textit{Annual Depreciation Expense} = \frac{\textit{Original Cost less Salvage Value}}{\textit{Useful Life}}$$

⇨ **Original Cost** is original cost of the asset.

⇨ **Salvage (Residual) Value** is the physical asset's estimated salvage / disposal / residual / trade-in value at the time of disposal. Original cost minus salvage value is often referred to as the depreciable cost.

⇨ **Useful Life** is total amount of time (usually in years) the asset is expected to remain in service. Useful life varies by asset types (asset classes).

Exercise: Depreciation

➡ A tire maker spends $100,000 in 2004 to acquire a piece of manufacturing equipment that is expected to be productive for the next five years.

➡ In 2009, the tire maker expects to sell it for $20,000.

➡ Calculate the annual depreciation expense using the straight-line depreciation method.

DEPRECIATION EXPENSE

Calculating Depreciation Expense: Straight-Line Depreciation Method

Solution: Depreciation

Annual depreciation expense =

$$\frac{\text{Original Cost} - \text{Salvage Value}}{\text{Useful Life}} = \frac{\$100,000 - \$20,000}{5} = \mathbf{\$16,000}$$

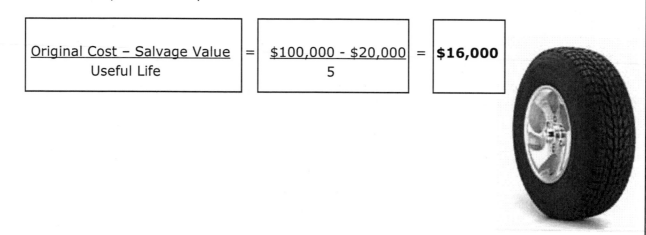

DEPRECIATION EXPENSE

Calculating Depreciation Expense: Accelerated Depreciation Method

➜ We just finished an example using the straight-line depreciation method.

➜ In practice, however, some assets (such as a car) lose more value in the beginning of their useful life than in the end. Companies may account for this by using an accelerated depreciation method.

➜ The two most common types of accelerated depreciation methods are:
    I.   Sum-of-the-Years' Digits (SYD)
    II.   Double-Declining Balance (DDB)

Calculating Depreciation Expense: Sum-of-the-Years' Digits (SYD) Method

➜ Sum-of-the-Years' Digits (SYD) method allows depreciation to be recorded based on a reversed scale of the total of digits for the years of useful life.

Depreciation in year z   = $\dfrac{(n-z+1)}{SYD} \times (\text{Original Cost} - \text{Salvage Value})$

⇨ Where $SYD = n(n+1)/2$ reflects the summation over the depreciable life of n years

⇨ n = useful life in years

⇨ z = current year

➜ Recall the previous example of straight-line depreciation, where a tire maker spends $100,000 in 2004 to acquire a piece of manufacturing equipment that is expected to be productive for the next five years, with an expected salvage value of $20,000. Let's instead apply the SYD method:

⇨ $SYD = n(n+1)/2 = (5)(5 + 1)/2 = 15$

⇨ Depreciation in year 1 = 5/15 x $80,000= $26,667

⇨ Depreciation in year 2 = 4/15 x $80,000 = $21,333

Exercise: Depreciation

⇨ Using the same methodology, complete the depreciation schedule in this example for years 3-5

DEPRECIATION EXPENSE

Calculating Depreciation Expense: Sum-of-the-Years' Digits Method

Solution: Depreciation

Year	Depreciation Rate (SYD)	Depreciable Cost (Original Cost – Salvage Value)	Depreciation (SYD x Depreciable Cost)	Book Value
0	-	$80,000	$0	$100,000
1	5/15	80,000	26,667	73,333
2	4/15	80,000	21,333	52,000
3	3/15	80,000	16,000	36,000
4	2/15	80,000	10,667	25,333
5	1/15	80,000	5,333	20,000

DEPRECIATION EXPENSE

Calculating Depreciation Expense: Double-Declining-Balance (DDB)

➔ Double-declining-balance method allows depreciation to be recorded at twice the rate of depreciation under straight-line method.

Depreciation in year z $\quad=\quad \dfrac{2}{n} \times$ (Original Cost – Accumulated Depreciation)

⇨ Where accumulated depreciation is the summation of all depreciation already recorded from the use of the asset.

⇨ n = useful life in years

Exercise: Depreciation

⇨ Using the previous example ($100,000 equipment with an expected life of 5 years and a salvage value of $20,000), complete the depreciation schedule for each of the years using DDB depreciation method.

DEPRECIATION EXPENSE

Calculating Depreciation Expense: Double-Declining-Balance (DDB)

Solution: Depreciation

Year	Beginning Book Value	Depreciable Rate (DDB)	Depreciation (Rate x Book Value)	Ending Book Value
0	$100,000	-	$0	$100,000
1	100,000	2/5	40,000	60,000
2	60,000	2/5	24,000	36,000
3	36,000	2/5	14,400	21,600
4	21,600		800	20,800
5	20.800		800	20,000

⇨ Note that in this example, DDB method was abandoned after year 3 since depreciation cannot decrease the book value of an asset below its salvage value. At this point, a company would be allowed to switch to straight-line depreciation method, and to depreciate the remaining $1,600 ($21,600 – $20,000) of an asset's depreciable cost over its remaining life (in this case, 2 years).

INCOME STATEMENT

DEPRECIATION EXPENSE

Depreciation methods compared

➜ Straight-line and accelerated depreciation methods result in the same total depreciable cost over the estimated useful life of an asset.

➜ The major difference between all of these methods is the timing of depreciation. Since depreciation is a tax-deductible expense, these timing differences have real tax implications for companies.

Year	Straight-Line	Sum-of-the-Years' Digits (SYD)	Double-Declining Balance (DDB)
0	$0	$0	$0
1	16,000	26,667	40,000
2	16,000	21,333	24,000
3	16,000	16,000	14,400
4	16,000	10,667	800
5	16,000	5,333	800
Total Depreciation	**$80,000**	**$80,000**	**$80,000**

AMORTIZATION

Definition

→ Amortization is the systematic allocation of the cost of acquired intangible assets over a period of time that these assets are expected to be in service and help generate revenue for a company.

→ Conceptually similar to depreciation and often lumped in with depreciation as Depreciation & Amortization (D&A).

→ When a company acquires an intangible asset from which it expects to generate benefits over future periods, the cost of that asset is not simply recognized during the year it was acquired. Instead, it is spread over that particular asset's useful life in the form of amortization expense in order to match the timing of the cost of the asset with its expected revenue generation.

Intangible assets include:
➲ Brand
➲ Franchise
➲ Trademarks
➲ Patents
➲ Customer Lists
➲ Licenses
➲ Goodwill

What about internally-generated intangible assets?
➲ The value of internally-developed intangibles cannot be accurately quantified, recorded, and therefore amortized (think back to Coke, GE, Microsoft).

INCOME STATEMENT

AMORTIZATION

Amortization is a "non-cash" expense (like depreciation)

➔ Amortization expense does not depict any actual cash outflow (payment)

What is the difference between depreciation and amortization?

➔ Depreciation is associated with fixed (physical) assets

➔ Amortization is associated with acquired intangible (not physical) assets

---

Exercise: Amortization

Which of the following need to be amortized, depreciated, or neither?

1. Automobile

2. Power plant

3. Acquired company's brand name

4. Brand name of an internally-generated business

5. A piece of land used to build a warehouse

AMORTIZATION

Solution: Amortization

The following need to be amortized, depreciated, or neither:

1.	Automobile	**depreciate**
2.	Power plant	**depreciate**
3.	Acquired company's brand name	**amortize**
4.	Brand name of an internally generated business	**neither**
5.	A piece of land used to build a warehouse	**neither**

Summary

➔ Amortization is a systematic expensing of costs of acquired intangible (not physical) assets.

➔ Amortization is a non-cash expense.

➔ Conceptually similar to depreciation and is often lumped with it under the Depreciation & Amortization (D&A) line item.

Intangibles – what is amortizable?

⊃ **Internally-developed intangibles:** value cannot be accurately assigned; they cannot be amortized.

⊃ **Acquired intangible assets:** value assigned as part of the transaction; amortization possible.

⊃ **Goodwill:** amortization abandoned after 2001 (see next page).

AMORTIZATION

Goodwill Amortization

→ Goodwill (recorded on the balance sheet) is the amount by which the purchase price for a company exceeds its fair market value (FMV), representing the "intangible" value stemming from the acquired company's business name, customer relations, employee morale.

Goodwill not amortized after 2001

→ Before December 15, 2001: goodwill on the balance sheet was amortized on the income statement under U.S. GAAP.

→ After December 15, 2001: Under a FASB ruling (SFAS 142), goodwill is no longer amortized on the income statement.

Big-Time acquires Johnny's Interiors

⮑ The fair market value of a local New York furniture company, Johnny's Interiors, is determined to be $5 million in 2003.

⮑ A national furniture company, Big-Time Furniture, believes that under its proven management and expertise, Johnny's Interiors would be worth much more than the fair market value (FMV) implies and thus decides to acquire Johnny's Interiors for $8 million, $3 million above the fair market value.

⮑ The $3 million Big-Time paid above the FMV is recorded as goodwill on its balance sheet.

INCOME STATEMENT

INTEREST EXPENSE

Definition

➜ Interest payments the company pays for its outstanding borrowings.

➜ Just as the interest we pay on credit cards or a car loan, corporations must make regular interest payments (interest expense) on debt owed to banks or other lenders.

⤴ Interest Expense is often presented on the income statement as Net Interest Expense.

⤴ Net Interest Expense accounts for the interest income a company earns from its cash and investment holdings (just like the interest income we make off of our savings or money-market bank accounts).

Exercise: Interest Expense

1. At the start of 2004, a firm decides to take out a $100,000 10-year loan, which at that time, has an interest rate of 5%. Calculate how much interest expense this company would record for the entire year, assuming it takes out this loan on January 1, 2004?

> A. 50,000
> B. 5,000
> C. 10,000
> D. 500

2. How much interest expense would the same firm record at the end of 2004 if it took out this loan on March 31, 2004?

> A. 37,534
> B. 3,753
> C. 7,506
> D. 375

INTEREST EXPENSE

Solution: Interest Expense

1.

      A.   50,000

      B.   5,000 $100,000 * 5% = $5,000

      C.   10,000

      D.   500

2.

      A.   37,534

      B.   3,753 $100,000 * 5% * 274/365

      C.   7,506

      D.   375

INCOME STATEMENT

INTEREST INCOME

Definition

➜ A company's income from its cash holdings and investments (stocks, bonds, and savings accounts). It is often not separately identified on the income statement, but rather embedded within the Net Interest Expense line.

OTHER NON-OPERATING INCOME

Definition

➜ A company's income from its non-core operating activities (gain on sale of asset or business, investment in affiliates, minority interest).

INCOME TAX EXPENSE

Definition

➜ The amount of taxes based on the pre-tax income a company owes to the government.

➜ Effective Tax Rate (GAAP) $= \dfrac{\text{Tax Expense}}{\text{Pre-Tax Income}}$

INCOME STATEMENT

EQUITY INCOME IN AFFILIATES

➜ Many companies have influential, but non-controlling investments in other firms (typically between 20%-50% ownership). They will account for their equity ownership (share of the investee's earnings minus any distributed dividends[1]) as "Equity in affiliates" on their income statement.

> **Equity in Affiliates = [% Investment in Affiliates] x [Affiliate Net Income – Dividends]**

Exercise: Equity Income in Affiliates

⇨ Company A owns 20% of company B, which just reported net income of $10 million and dividends of $2 million. What should company A record in the "Equity income in affiliates" line item?

---

[1] See page 93 for a definition of dividends

EQUITY INCOME IN AFFILIATES

Solution: Equity Income in Affiliates

Income in Affiliates = [% Investment in Affiliates] x [Affiliate Net Income – Dividends]

Income in affiliates = 20% x ($10 million - $2 million) = $1.6 million

Company A should record $1.6 million in the "Equity income in affiliates" line item

MINORITY INTEREST

➔ When companies have an influential and controlling investment in another company (typically between 50%-100% ownership), they will account for their majority ownership using consolidated method of accounting:

    ⇨ Consolidated simply means that financial reports of the parent company contain all financial information (revenues, net income, etc.) of all businesses in which it holds 50%-100%.

➔ Since companies often hold a majority ownership of less than 100%, they must account for minority interest i.e. the remaining minority stake owned by other shareholders.

Exercise: Minority Interest

⇨ Company A owns 80% of company B, which just reported net income of $10 million and dividends of $2 million.

1. How much of company B's earnings will company A record under the consolidated method of accounting?

2. What should company A record in the "Minority Interest" line item?

MINORITY INTEREST

Solution: Minority Interest

---

1. Since Company A owns 80% of company B, it will record all of the latter's earnings minus distributed dividends under the consolidated method:
   - ⇨ $10 million - $2 million = $8 million

2. Minority interest must reflect the 20% stake of company B not owned by company A:

   - ⇨ 20% x (Net income from company B – dividends from company B) =
   - ⇨ 20% x ($10 million - $2 million) =
   - ⇨ 20% of $8 million = $1.6 million

INCOME STATEMENT

NET INCOME

→ Net Income is the final measure of profitability on the income statement. It represents income after all expenses have been paid out.

→ Net Income is the difference between the company's revenues and expenses (COGS, SG&A, D&A, Interest, Other and Taxes) i.e. its "bottom line".

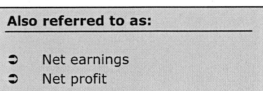

Also referred to as:

⊃ Net earnings
⊃ Net profit
⊃ "Bottom line"

SHARES OUTSTANDING

→ Represent the number of shares of common stock outstanding. One share of common stock represents one unit of ownership of a public company.

→ The number of shares outstanding represents capital invested by the firm's shareholders. Shares that have been issued, but subsequently repurchased by the company are called treasury stock and they are no longer outstanding (we'll discuss why a company may choose to repurchase its shares at a later point).

1. You own 100 shares of a public company
2. It has 100 million shares outstanding
⊃ You own 0.000001% of that firm

→ Owners of these shares (shareholders) are generally entitled to vote on the selection of directors and other important matters in proportion with the number of shares they own (i.e. 100 shares = 100 votes) as well as to receive dividends on their holdings.

Shares Outstanding = Shares Issued – Treasury Stock

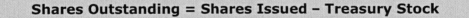

SHARES OUTSTANDING

➔ Shares outstanding are reflected on the income statement in 2 line items:

    1. Weighted average basic shares outstanding

        ⇨ Shares of common stock outstanding

    2. Weighted average diluted shares outstanding

        ⇨ Shares of common stock outstanding *plus*: potential shares that may result from the conversion of other securities into common stock, and thus *dilute* the share base (increase the number of shares outstanding).

        ⇨ Securities that can be converted into common stock include:

            1. Stock options & warrants (the right to buy shares at predetermined price)

            2. Convertible preferred stock

            3. Convertible debt

➔ Since the total number of shares outstanding fluctuates as shares from other securities are converted or the company repurchases shares, companies usually show the number of shares outstanding on the income statement as weighted average of the amount of shares outstanding during the period of the income statement (quarter or year).

➔ **What is the relevance of shares outstanding?**

    ⇨ While the absolute level of a company's profitability (net income) is important, its per-share amount is a more useful measure for comparison and analysis.

SHARES OUTSTANDING

Exercise: Shares Outstanding

⇨ At year-end 2004, basic shares outstanding were 145 million. During 2005, the following things happened:

⇨ 1/26/05 – company repurchased 2 million shares
⇨ 3/21/05 – options were converted into 5 million common shares

⇨ **Calculate 2005 weighted average shares outstanding and the 2005 year-end shares outstanding**

SHARES OUTSTANDING

Solution: Shares Outstanding

1. **Calculate 2005 weighted average shares outstanding:**
   ⇨ Start of 2005: 145 million shares for 25 days (until January 26, 2005)

   ⇨ 2 million share repurchase: 143 million shares for 54 days (1/26/05-3/21/05)

   ⇨ 5 million option-to-stock conversion: 148 million shares for 285 days (3/21/05-12/31/05)

$$\frac{(145 \times 25) + (143 \times 54) + (148 \times 285)}{365 \text{ days}} = 146.65 \text{ million shares}$$

2. **Calculate 2005 year-end shares outstanding:**
   ⇨ 148 million shares

Number of shares outstanding varies across firms:

➜ During its 2004 fiscal year, Microsoft had diluted weighted average shares outstanding of almost 10.9 billion.

➜ During 2004, ExxonMobil had diluted weighted average shares outstanding of over 6.5 billion.

➜ In 2004, McDonald's had diluted weighted average shares outstanding of almost 1,274 million.

➜ In 2004, Amazon.com had diluted weighted average shares outstanding of almost 425 million.

INCOME STATEMENT

COMMON DIVIDENDS

→ Dividends represent a portion of a company's net income that is returned to shareholders, typically on a quarterly basis, in the form of cash.

→ Dividend policy is set by the Board of Directors, is reviewed regularly, and is disclosed in the company's financial statements.

During 2004 Fiscal Year:
- ExxonMobil's quarterly cash dividend was $0.27 per share.
- Microsoft's was $0.32 per share.
- Amazon.com pays no dividends.

PREFERRED DIVIDENDS

→ Preferred dividends are paid before common dividends to the holders of preferred stock, which has special rights and takes priority over common stock.

→ Common stock dividends are then paid out of the remaining net income usually referred to as Earnings Available to Common Shareholders.

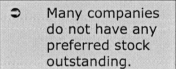

- Many companies do not have any preferred stock outstanding.

93

EARNINGS PER SHARE (EPS)

➜ Earnings per Share (EPS) is a popular profitability ratio, measured as the portion of a company's earnings allocated to each outstanding share of common stock.

EPS is calculated as:

1. Basic EPS

   ⇨ <u>Net income available to common shareholders</u>
   Basic weighted average shares outstanding

2. Diluted EPS

   ⇨ <u>Net income available to common shareholders</u>
   Diluted weighted average shares outstanding

➜ Diluted shares include the impact of potentially dilutive securities that expand the share base, so diluted EPS will almost always be smaller than basic EPS.

➲ It is often referred to as net income per share or simply EPS.

➲ Both Basic and Diluted EPS are usually presented on the income statement.

Exercise: EPS

⇨ A food retailer has $15 million in net earnings. It has 5 million shares of common stock outstanding and stock options that can be convertible into 2 million shares.

Calculate

1. Basic EPS

2. Diluted EPS

EARNINGS PER SHARE (EPS)

Solution: EPS

---

1. Basic EPS = $15 million / 5 million = $3.00

2. Diluted EPS = $15 million / 7 million = $2.14

⇨ **Notice that Diluted EPS < Basic EPS**

NONRECURRING ITEMS

➔ Some events that generate gains or losses are not expected to recur:

⇨ Losses from natural disaster
⇨ Losses from major corporate restructuring
⇨ Income for legal settlement
⇨ Asset write-downs
⇨ Losses from discontinued operations
⇨ Gains or losses from an accounting change
⇨ Other

➔ Whether or not non-recurring items will be reported pre-tax (before net income) or after-tax (after net income) carries important analytical implications.

➔ Placement on the income statement depends on the nature and classification of the nonrecurring items.

➔ Under GAAP, classification of nonrecurring items is broken down into four categories:

⇨ Unusual or Infrequent Items	reported pre-tax
⇨ Extraordinary Items	reported after-tax
⇨ Discontinued Operations	reported after-tax
⇨ Accounting Changes	reported after-tax

INCOME STATEMENT

NONRECURRING ITEMS

1. Unusual or infrequent items

➔ Transactions that are unusual in nature *or* infrequent, but not both

➔ Such transactions may include:

⇨ Gains (losses) from the sale of the company's assets, business segments
⇨ Gains (losses) from asset impairments, write-offs, and restructuring
⇨ Losses from lawsuits
⇨ Provision for environmental remediation

➔ Reported pre-tax, so for the purposes of financial analysis, unusual items must be excluded from future earnings when forecasting them.

➔ Unusual or infrequent items pose a challenge for financial analysts because they can skew the picture of operating performance, which in turn can hamper analysts' ability to make forecasts for future operating performance.

⇨ Management has discretion over how to classify operating items.
⇨ Unusual or infrequent items are not always clearly labeled.
⇨ They may be shown as separate items on the income statement if they are material ("Gain on Sale of Assets" line) or may be buried within operating items.
⇨ In either case, all unusual or infrequent items are reported pre-tax and therefore affect net income.
⇨ Create potential for manipulation.

INCOME STATEMENT

NONRECURRING ITEMS

1. Unusual or infrequent items

Illustration: Unusual or infrequent items

You calculate pre-tax income from a company's income statement as follows:

Year	2000	2001	2002	2003
Revenues	$500	$600	$720	$860
- COGS (w/D&A)	$200	$240	$300	$400
- SG&A	$215	$240	$300	$330
- Interest	$5	$5	$5	$5
- Other expenses	--	--	--	$70
Pre-tax income	**$80**	**$95**	**$115**	**$55**
% growth		*18.8%*	*21.1%*	*(52.2%)*

Big drop!

➜ 2003 seemed to be an unusually weak year.

➜ A company's footnotes reveal that it recorded an unusual $70m loss from an asset write-down buried within other expenses.

➜ Should analysts build future year projections off of the deeply depressed $55m pre-tax income or should they adjust 2003 to exclude the write-down, bringing pre-tax income back up from $55m to $125m? They should exclude the write-down as it is an unusual item.

NONRECURRING ITEMS

1. Unusual or infrequent items

Figure 16. Unusual or infrequent items

ChevronTexaco 2004 Income Statement

	Year ended December 31		
	2004	2003	2002
REVENUES AND OTHER INCOME			
Sales and other operating revenues [1,2]	$ 150,865	$ 119,575	$ 98,340
Income (loss) from equity affiliates	2,582	1,029	(25)
Other income	1,853	308	222
Gain from exchange of Dynegy preferred stock	–	365	–
TOTAL REVENUES AND OTHER INCOME	155,300	121,277	98,537
COSTS AND OTHER DEDUCTIONS			
Purchased crude oil and products [2]	94,419	71,310	57,051
Operating expenses	9,832	8,500	7,795
Selling, general and administrative expenses	4,557	4,440	4,155
Exploration expenses	697	570	591
Depreciation, depletion and amortization	4,935	5,326	5,169
Taxes other than on income [1]	19,818	17,901	16,682
Interest and debt expense	406	474	565
Minority interests	85	80	57
Write-down of investments in Dynegy Inc.	–	–	1,796
Merger-related expenses	–	–	576
TOTAL COSTS AND OTHER DEDUCTIONS	134,749	108,601	94,437
INCOME FROM CONTINUING OPERATIONS BEFORE INCOME TAX EXPENSE	20,551	12,676	4,100
INCOME TAX EXPENSE	7,517	5,294	2,998
INCOME FROM CONTINUING OPERATIONS	13,034	7,382	1,102
INCOME FROM DISCONTINUED OPERATIONS	294	44	30
INCOME BEFORE CUMULATIVE EFFECT OF CHANGES IN ACCOUNTING PRINCIPLES	$ 13,328	$ 7,426	$ 1,132
Cumulative effect of changes in accounting principles	–	(196)	–
NET INCOME	$ 13,328	$ 7,230	$ 1,132
PER-SHARE OF COMMON STOCK [3]			
INCOME FROM CONTINUING OPERATIONS			
– BASIC	$ 6.16	$ 3.55	$ 0.52
– DILUTED	$ 6.14	$ 3.55	$ 0.52
INCOME FROM DISCONTINUED OPERATIONS			
– BASIC	$ 0.14	$ 0.02	$ 0.01
– DILUTED	$ 0.14	$ 0.02	$ 0.01
CUMULATIVE EFFECT OF CHANGES IN ACCOUNTING PRINCIPLES			
– BASIC	$ –	$ (0.09)	$ –
– DILUTED	$ –	$ (0.09)	$ –
NET INCOME			
– BASIC	$ 6.30	$ 3.48	$ 0.53
– DILUTED	$ 6.28	$ 3.48	$ 0.53
[1] Includes consumer excise taxes:	$ 7,968	$ 7,095	$ 7,006
[2] Includes amounts in revenues for buy/sell contracts (associated costs are in "Purchased crude oil and products"). See Note 16 on page FS-41:	$ 18,650	$ 14,246	$ 7,963

[3] All periods reflect a two-for-one stock split effected as a 100 percent stock dividend in September 2004.
See accompanying Notes to the Consolidated Financial Statements.

2. Discontinued Operations

➔ Represent physically and operationally distinct segments or assets that a company has sold or in the process of divesting in the current year.

➔ Reported net of taxes on a separate line called "Income (Loss) from Discontinued Operations" to distinguish it from core earnings "Income (Loss) from Continuing Operations."

⇨ Disclosed on the income statement after income from continuing operations, but before extraordinary items.

➔ Criteria in determining what constitutes discontinued operations is not clear.

3. Extraordinary Items

➔ Results that are unusual AND infrequent AND material in amount

➔ Such transactions may include:

⇨ Gains (losses) on the extinguishment (early repayment) of debt

⇨ Uninsured losses from natural disasters

⇨ Losses from expropriation of assets by foreign governments

⇨ Gains/losses from passage of new law

➔ Reported on the income statement net of taxes (after net income) from continuing operations.

NONRECURRING ITEMS

4. Accounting Changes

→ Represent changes in a company's accounting methodology governing the reporting of its financial statements.

→ Reported net of taxes on a separate line item following extraordinary items.

→ Types of accounting changes include:

<u>A. Changes Applied to New Transactions</u>
⇨ New transactions occur only after the accounting change takes place
⇨ No adjustments to current financial statements are required
⇨ Ex: Applying a different depreciation method to new assets

<u>B. Changes in Estimates</u>
⇨ Can be associated with useful lives and salvage value of depreciable assets as well as value of uncollectible revenue (recall Bad Debt Expense is an estimate).
⇨ Changes are made only in the affected (present and/or future) period(s); past results remain as originally reported.

<u>C. Retroactive Changes in Accounting Principles</u>
⇨ If the company chooses to apply newly adopted accounting principles retroactively (to the past results), the impact of this change on prior periods is shown as a separate item on the income statement called "Cumulative effect of the accounting change on prior periods."

Figure 17. Accounting changes

McDonald's
2004 Income Statement

Note the accounting change

Consolidated statement of income

IN MILLIONS, EXCEPT PER SHARE DATA	Years ended December 31, 2004	2003	2002
REVENUES			
Sales by Company-operated restaurants	$14,223.8	$12,795.4	$11,499.6
Revenues from franchised and affiliated restaurants	4,840.9	4,345.1	3,906.1
Total revenues	19,064.7	17,140.5	15,405.7
OPERATING COSTS AND EXPENSES			
Company-operated restaurant expenses			
Food & paper	4,852.7	4,314.8	3,917.4
Payroll & employee benefits	3,726.3	3,411.4	3,078.2
Occupancy & other operating expenses	3,520.8	3,279.8	2,911.0
Franchised restaurants-occupancy expenses	1,003.2	937.7	840.1
Selling, general & administrative expenses	1,980.0	1,833.0	1,712.8
Other operating expense, net	441.2	531.6	833.3
Total operating costs and expenses	15,524.2	14,308.3	13,292.8
Operating income	3,540.5	2,832.2	2,112.9
Interest expense-net of capitalized interest of $4.1, $7.8 and $14.3	358.4	388.0	374.1
Nonoperating (income) expense, net	(26.3)	97.8	76.7
Income before provision for income taxes and cumulative effect of accounting changes	3,202.4	2,346.4	1,662.1
Provision for income taxes	923.9	838.2	670.0
Income before cumulative effect of accounting changes	2,278.5	1,508.2	992.1
Cumulative effect of accounting changes, net of tax benefits of $9.4 and $17.6		(36.8)	(98.6)
Net income	$ 2,278.5	$ 1,471.4	$ 893.5
Per common share-basic:			
Income before cumulative effect of accounting changes	$ 1.81	$ 1.19	$ .79
Cumulative effect of accounting changes		(.03)	(.08)
Net income	$ 1.81	$ 1.16	$ .70
Per common share-diluted:			
Income before cumulative effect of accounting changes	$ 1.79	$ 1.18	$ .77
Cumulative effect of accounting changes		(.03)	(.07)
Net income	$ 1.79	$ 1.15	$ .70
Dividends per common share	$ .55	$ .40	$ .24
Weighted-average shares outstanding-basic	1,259.7	1,269.8	1,273.1
Weighted-average shares outstanding-diluted	1,273.7	1,276.5	1,291.5

NONRECURRING ITEMS

Summary

Type	Classification	Description	Analytical implications
Unusual or infrequent	**Above the line** Reported pre-tax before net income from continuing operations.	Events that are either unusual or infrequent (but not both). Examples of unusual or infrequent item are restructuring charges, one-time write-offs, gains/losses on sale of assets.	Management often "buries" these within normal operating items (COGS, SG&A, or Other Operating Expenses), so it is often difficult to identify these items. Management usually identifies these items in the annual report footnotes and the MD&A sections. Non-recurring charges tend to also appear in press releases. Companies have more flexibility and thus tend to go into more detail about non-recurring charges on their unaudited press releases. Recognize that non-recurring charges allow for management discretion and judgment, and thus, manipulation, so be aware of this in determining whether some items should not be excluded.
Extraordinary	**Below the line** Reported net of tax after net income from continuing operations.	Events that are both unusual *and* infrequent *and* material in amount. Examples are gains/losses from early retirement of debt, uninsured losses from natural disasters, loss from expropriation of assets, gains/losses from passage of new law.	Since extraordinary items are reported after net income, they do not affect operating income. Still, an analyst may still want to review these to determine whether some extraordinary items *should* be included above the line. Some management teams are more "prone" to extraordinary events.

NONRECURRING ITEMS

Summary

Type	Classification	Description	Analytical implications
Discontinued Operations	**Below the line** Reported net of tax after net income from continuing operations.	A physically and operationally distinct business that a company has decided to – but has not yet – disposed of, or has disposed of in the current year.	Companies identify income and losses from discontinued operations separately from the rest of the income statement, and must restate past income statements (which included the discontinued operations) to exclude the discontinued operations for comparability. Since discontinued operations are reported after net income, they do not affect operating income.
Accounting changes	**Below the line** Reported net of tax after net income from continuing operations.	Any change in accounting methods.	Since accounting changes are reported after net income, they do not affect operating income and rarely have a cash flow impact. Prior financial statements need not be restated unless the accounting change is a change in inventory accounting method, change to or from full-cost method, change to or from the % of completion method, or any change just prior to an IPO.

EBITDA

→ EBITDA (earnings before interest, taxes, depreciation and amortization) is a measure of profitability (like net income and gross profit) designed to allow analysts to compare profitability between companies and industries.

→ EBITDA excludes the effects of financing and accounting decisions.

→ Disregards the companies' capital investments (fixed assets) and associated (non-cash) depreciation and amortization expenses.

Sample Income Statement	
Revenues	$100
- Cost of Goods Sold	20
- SG&A (incl. R&D)	15
EBITDA	**65**
- D&A	10
EBIT	55
- Interest Expense	5
-Taxes	20
Net Income	30

EBITDA

Sales – COGS – SG&A – R&D

Or

Net Income + Taxes + Interest Expense + D&A

→ EBITDA facilitates an "apples-to-apples" comparison between companies using different depreciation methods and assumptions.

→ Allows comparisons between high fixed-asset industries (such as real estate, transportation, and utilities) and those in service industries with relatively low level of fixed assets (software, financial services).

EBITDA

EBITDA is a popular measure of a company's financial performance

→ Does not take into account a company's level of interest expense (payment on borrowings), and therefore "levels the field" between companies with significant financial leverage (debt) and those with little/any.

→ Does not include the effect of taxes, which as we will learn later in the book, are subject to change based on different accounting methods companies use, as permissible by GAAP, and do not reflect operating profitability.

→ By eliminating the effects of financial leverage (debt), taxes, and capital investments (D&A expenses), EBITDA can be viewed as a good indicator of core operating profitability of a company.

EBITDA is used widely in analysis

➲ EBITDA became a popular financial metric since leveraged buyouts (LBOs) in the 1980s, when it was used to indicate the ability of a company to service debt by LBO firms and lenders.

➲ EBITDA/Sales ratio, for example, can be used to find the most "efficient" operator in a particular industry.

➲ EBITDA can be used to analyze and compare profitability trends of different companies across industries over time.

➲ Through such ratios as Debt/EBITDA and EBITDA/Interest Expense, EBITDA is a popular proxy for a company's ability to take on debt.

EBITDA

EBITDA has several shortcomings:

1. Not a good measure of cash flow

➔ Does not take into account a company's:

⇨ Debt payments (cash out)

⇨ Capital expenditures (investments in fixed assets – cash out)

⇨ Working capital (day-to-day cash requirements needed for a company's ongoing operations)

2. Can be manipulated to show a desired level of profitability

➔ Since it ignores debt payments, taxes and capital expenditures, EBITDA can be used by companies as their primary level of profitability. However, this can be misleading if after taking into account those three "obligations", companies may instead be losing money.

➔ WorldCom overstated cash flow by booking $3.8 billion in operating expenses as capital expenses.

3. Inappropriate metric to use in various capital-intensive industries

➔ Certain industries such as cable and telecom, transportation, and energy are very capital-intensive. Using EBITDA metric, which ignores significant amount of capital expenditures undertaken by companies, may be inappropriate for these industries.

The final word on EBITDA

EBITDA is a very useful measure of profitability. However, it must be used in the analysis of a company's financial health with a full awareness of its limitations and potential for misrepresentation.

EBITDA

Exercise: EBITDA

⇨   A computer manufacturer sells 10,000 computers per year at a price of $1,000 per unit.

⇨   It costs the manufacturer $200 to produce and ship each computer.

⇨   The manufacturer spends:
- ⇨ $200,000 in office supplies.
- ⇨ $600,000 on employee salaries.
- ⇨ $150,000 on new technology research.

Calculate EBITDA

INCOME STATEMENT

EBITDA

Solution: EBITDA

Revenue:	$10,000,000
COGS:	- 2,000,000
Gross Profit:	8,000,000
SG&A:	- 800,000
R&D:	- 150,000
EBITDA	**$7,050,000**

INCOME STATEMENT

EBIT

→ EBIT (earnings before interest and taxes), measures a company's core profitability based on industry factors, without taking into effect a firm's financial leverage or taxes.

→ EBIT/Sales ratio is usually referred to as Operating Profit Margin and is used to find the most "efficient" operator in a particular industry.

→ EBIT has most of the EBITDA shortcomings discussed earlier:

1. It is not a good measure of cash flow
   ⇨ Does not take into account debt payments and working capital
   ⇨ Includes D&A – non-cash items
2. EBIT can be used as an accounting gimmick

→ Note that since EBIT does take into account D&A expense (stemming from capital investments and acquisitions), it avoids the limitation of EBITDA arising in capital-intensive industries.

Sample Income Statement

Revenues	$100
- Cost of Goods Sold	20
- SG&A (inc. R&D)	15
EBITDA	65
- D&A	10
EBIT	**55**
- Interest Expense	5
-Taxes	20
Net Income	30

EBIT (Operating Profit or Operating Income)

Revenues – COGS – SG&A – R&D – D&A
Or
Net Income + Taxes + Interest Expense

INCOME STATEMENT

SUMMARY

➔ The income statement is a summary of a company's profitability over a certain period of time.

⇨ Profitability is the difference between revenues and expenses generated by a company's activities.

⇨ Revenues are recognized when an economic exchange occurs, and expenses associated with a product are matched during the same period as revenue generated from that product.

⇨ Special care must be taken to distinguish operating expenses (stemming from core activities) from non-operating costs (arising from peripheral transactions) in arriving at a company's net income.

⇨ Net income is an important indicator of a company's operating performance.

STANDARD LINE ITEMS IN THE INCOME STATEMENT

Line Item	Description	Notes
Net Revenues	Total dollar payment for goods and services that are credited to an income statement over a particular time period.	
Cost of Goods Sold	Cost of Goods sold represents a company's direct cost of manufacture (for manufacturers) or procurement (for merchandisers) of a good or service that the company sells to generate revenue.	May include unusual or infrequent items that need to be excluded
Gross Profit	Revenues - Cost of Goods Sold	
SG&A	Operating costs not directly associated with the production or procurement of the product or service that the company sells to generate revenue. Payroll, wages, commissions, meal and travel expenses, stationary, advertising, and marketing expenses fall under this line item.	May include unusual or infrequent items that need to be excluded
R&D	A company's activities that are directed at developing new products or procedures.	May be buried in SG&A
EBITDA	Gross Profit - SG&A - R&D. EBITDA is a popular measure of a company's financial performance.	
D&A	The allocation of cost over a fixed (depreciation) or intangible (amortization) asset's useful life in order to match the timing of the cost of the asset with when it is expected to generate revenue benefits.	May be buried in COGS
Other Operating Expenses / Income	Any operating expenses not allocated to COGS, SG&A, R&D, D&A.	May include unusual or infrequent items that need to be excluded
EBIT	EBITCA - D&A	
Interest Expense	Interest expense is the amount the company has to pay on debt owed. This could be to bondholders or to banks. Interest expense subtracted from EBIT equals earnings before taxes (EBT).	Usually Net Interest on the income statement - net of Interest Income
Interest Income	A company's income from its cash holdings and investments (stocks, bonds, and savings accounts)	Usually netted against Interest Expense
Unusual or Infrequent Income / Expenses	Gain (loss) on sale of assets, disposal of a business segment, impairment charge, write-offs, restructuring costs.	Likely need to be excluded
Income Tax Expense	The tax liability a company reports on the income statement	
Net Income	EBIT - Net Interest Expense - Other Nonoperating Income - Taxes	
Basic EPS	Net income / Basic Weighted Average Shares Outstanding	
Diluted EPS	Net income / Diluted Weighted Average Shares Outstanding	

Exercise: The Lemonade Stand

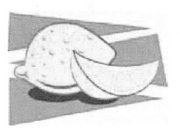

⇨ On January 1, 2004, you decide to enter a lemonade stand business. In order to buy all the required equipment and supplies to get started, you estimate that you will need $50, plus an extra $100 for cushion.

⇨ You open up a business checking account into which you put $100 of your own money and borrow $50 from the bank at a 10% annual interest rate.

⇨ You buy $20 worth of lemons and paper cups (just enough to make 100 cups of lemonade). You also buy a lemon squeezer and a lemonade stand for $30.

⇨ You estimate that both the lemon squeezer and lemonade stand will have a useful life of 3 years, upon which they will be obsolete and be thrown away (assume straight-line depreciation).

⇨ You operate the business for a year and sell 100 cups of lemonade for $1 each.

⇨ The cost of lemons and the paper cup required to make a cup of lemonade is $0.20.

⇨ In addition, you also hired an employee to help operate the stand and paid him $15 for the year.

⇨ Tax rate for the lemonade stand business is 40%.

⇨ The accounting period ends on 12/31/04.

⇨ **Create an income statement for the lemonade stand for 2004 based on this information**

⇨ Hint: much of the background information will not be reflected in the income statement – your ability to understand what activities of a company are recorded on its income statement and which are left out is the first step in identifying which of them belong in this financial statement.

Income Statement for the Lemonade Stand

Accounting Period

Revenue

Cost of goods sold

Selling, general & administrative expenses

Depreciation & amortization

EBIT

Net interest expense

Non-operating income / (expenses)

Taxes

Net income

Revenues: 100 cups sold at $1 a cup = $100.

COGS: For each cup sold, you paid $0.20 for the cup and lemons = $0.20 x 100 cups = $20.

SG&A: You paid your employee $15. This falls under the category SG&A. Note that if you decided to pay yourself a salary, or purchased supplies for bookkeeping or a sale banner to place above your lemonade stand, that would have also been categorized as SG&A.

D&A: The lemon squeezer and lemonade stand were $30, with a useful life of 3 years and no salvage value. The annual depreciation expense is calculated as $30 / 3 years = $10.

Interest Expense: Annual interest expense on a $50 bank loan with an annual interest rate of 10% is $50 x 10% = $5.

Taxes: Applying a tax rate of 40% to a company's pre-tax income of $50 results in taxes of $20.

Net income: Pretax income of $50 – income tax expense of $20 = $30.

January 1, 2004 to December 31, 2004

Income Statement	
Revenues	100
- Cost of Goods Sold	20
- SG&A	15
- D&A	10
EBIT	55
- Interest Expense	5
- Taxes	20
Net Income	30

Exercise: The Lemonade Stand (Continued)

Additionally during the period . . .

⇨   You earn $2 in interest income from your business account.

⇨   You are sued by a customer who slipped on your lemonade – you settle out of court for $5.

⇨   You take your lemonade public in an initial public offering and issue 100 shares of common stock.

⇨   **Modify the income statement for the lemonade stand for 2004 accordingly**

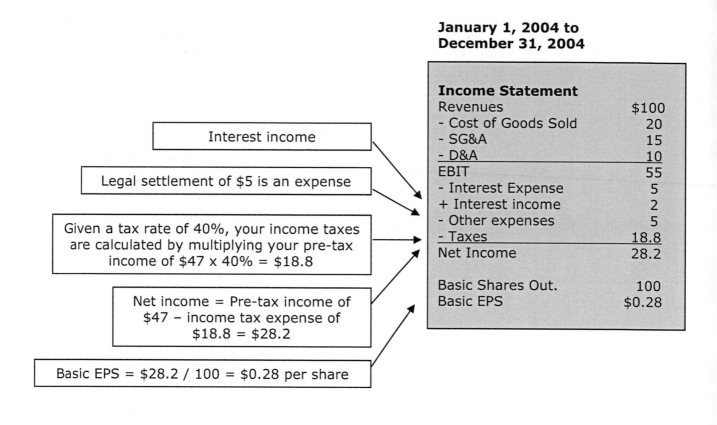

January 1, 2004 to December 31, 2004

Interest income

Legal settlement of $5 is an expense

Given a tax rate of 40%, your income taxes are calculated by multiplying your pre-tax income of $47 x 40% = $18.8

Net income = Pre-tax income of $47 – income tax expense of $18.8 = $28.2

Basic EPS = $28.2 / 100 = $0.28 per share

Income Statement	
Revenues	$100
- Cost of Goods Sold	20
- SG&A	15
- D&A	10
EBIT	55
- Interest Expense	5
+ Interest income	2
- Other expenses	5
- Taxes	18.8
Net Income	28.2
Basic Shares Out.	100
Basic EPS	$0.28

→ Note that as an analyst, you may decide that the $5 legal settlement is an unusual event and should be excluded when assessing the company's future earnings prospects.

→ As such, you would exclude the $5 expense, increasing pre-tax income. Accordingly, you would need to adjust taxes up to reflect the absence of the litigation expense.

CHAPTER 6

BALANCE SHEET

INTRODUCTION

➜ Recall that the income statement reports a company's revenues, expenses and profitability over a specified period of time.

➜ The balance sheet reports the company's resources (assets) and how those resources were funded (liabilities and shareholders' equity) on a particular date (end of the quarter, end of the year).

➜ The fundamental equation in Accounting is:

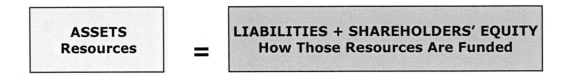

| ASSETS
Resources | **=** | LIABILITIES + SHAREHOLDERS' EQUITY
How Those Resources Are Funded |

Historical Cost & Conservatism Principle Revisited

➜ Recall that financial statements report company's resources – including most balance sheet items – at their historical (acquisition) cost.

➜ By not allowing assets to be overstated, the historical cost principle is an example of conservatism.

➜ Governed by the historical cost principle, the balance sheet does not report the true market value of a company – only its resources and funding at their historical cost.

Assets represent the company's resources

➔   To qualify as an asset, the following requirements must be met:

☑   A company must own the resource

☑   The resource must be of value

☑   The resource must have a quantifiable, measurable cost

Assets typically consist of (but are not always limited to):

ASSETS	
Cash and Cash Equivalents	Money held by the company in its bank accounts
Marketable Securities (Short-Term Investments)	Debt or equity securities held by the company
Accounts Receivable	Payment owed to a business by its customers for products and services already delivered to them
Inventories	Inventories represent any unfinished or finished goods that are waiting to be sold, and the direct costs associated with the production of these goods
Property, Plant & Equipment ("Fixed Assets")	Land, buildings, and machinery used in the manufacture of the company's services and products
Goodwill and Intangible Assets	Non-physical assets such as brands, patents, trademarks, and goodwill acquired by the company that have value based on the rights belonging to that company
Deferred Taxes	Potential future tax savings arising when taxes payable to the IRS are higher than those recorded on financial statements
Other ("Miscellaneous") Assets	Items that do not fit into other categories, such as pre-paid expenses, or some types of short or long-term investments

BALANCE SHEET

INTRODUCTION

Exercise: Identifying Assets

Which of the following accounts are assets for Microsoft?

❑ Cash

❑ An office building owned by Microsoft

❑ Microsoft's software inventories

❑ Microsoft's employees

❑ Microsoft's brand name

❑ Bill Gates' personal car

Solution: Identifying Assets

Which of the following accounts are assets for Microsoft?

☑ Cash

☑ An office building owned by Microsoft

☑ Microsoft's software inventories

☐ Microsoft's employees – value cannot be measured

☐ Microsoft's brand name – not acquired at measurable cost

☐ Bill Gates' personal car – not owned by company

BALANCE SHEET

INTRODUCTION

Liabilities and Shareholders' Equity represent the company's sources of funds i.e. how it pays for assets.

➔ Liabilities represent what the company owes to others:

  ☑ They must be measurable

  ☑ Their occurrence is probable

➔ Shareholders' Equity represents sources of funds through:

  1. Equity investment

  2. Retained earnings (what the company has earned through operations since its inception)

Liabilities and Shareholders' Equity typically consist of (but are not always limited to):

LIABILITIES

Accounts Payable	A company's obligations to suppliers for services and products already purchased from them, but which have not been paid. In other words, accounts payable represent the company's unpaid bills to its suppliers for services obtained on credit from them.
Notes Payable	Debt or equity securities held by the company
Current Portion of Long-Term Debt	Portion of debt with an overall maturity of more than a year; this portion is due within 12 months
Long-Term Debt	The company's borrowings with a maturity (full repayment) exceeding 12 months
Deferred Taxes	Potential future tax obligations arising when taxes payable to the IRS are lower than those recorded on financial statements
Minority Interest	Equity interest in the portion of the consolidated businesses that the company does not own

SHAREHOLDERS' EQUITY

Preferred Stock	Stock that has special rights and takes priority over common stock
Common Stock Par Value	Par value of units of ownership of a corporation
Additional Paid-In Capital (APIC)	Represents capital received by a company when its shares are sold above their par value
Treasury Stock	Common stock that had been issued and then reacquired (bought back) by a company
Retained Earnings	Total amount of earnings of a company since its inception minus dividends and losses (if any)

BALANCE SHEET

INTRODUCTION

Exercise: Identifying Liabilities

Which of the following accounts are liabilities for Microsoft?

❑ Funds owed to suppliers for purchases Microsoft made on credit

❑ Corporate debt

❑ The possibility that employees will strike

❑ A really bad employee

BALANCE SHEET

INTRODUCTION

Solution: Identifying Liabilities

Which of the following accounts are liabilities for Microsoft?

- ☑ Funds owed to suppliers for purchases Microsoft made on credit

- ☑ Corporate debt

- ☐ The possibility that employees will strike

- ☐ A really bad employee

The Lemonade Stand and the Accounting Equation

➜   Recalling the lemonade stand, you opened up a business checking account into which you put $100 of your own money and borrowed $50 from the bank, which agreed to lend it to you at a 10% annual interest rate.

➜   At its inception on January 1, 2004, what are the lemonade stand's assets (resources) and how were those assets funded (liabilities and shareholders' equity)?

Assets	= Total cash available to the business	=	$150
Liabilities	= Bank loan	=	$50
Shareholders' equity (SE)	= Your own money	=	$100

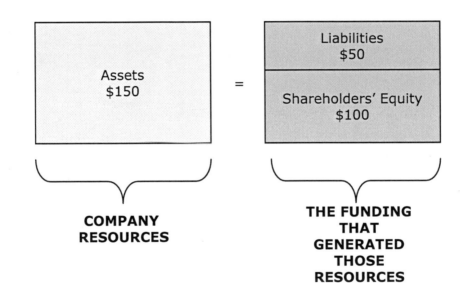

BALANCE SHEET

Balance Sheet

➜   Based on these transactions, the balance sheet would look as follows:

➜   Assets must equal Liabilities + Shareholders' Equity by definition. They are two sides of the same coin.

➜   When the lemonade stand's assets increased by $150, this was accompanied by a corresponding increase in liabilities and shareholders' equity.

➜   There had to be a source of cash (it had to come from somewhere).

➜   This is why the balance sheet must always balance.

Ending January 1, 2004

Balance Sheet	
Assets	
Cash	150
Accounts Receivable	0
Inventories	0
PP&E	0
Total Assets	150
Liabilities	
Accounts Payable	0
Debt	50
Total Liabilities	50
Shareholders' Equity	
Common Stock and APIC	100
Retained Earnings	0
Total SE	100

➜   In reality, companies have more assets than just cash.

  ⇨   Companies use cash to buy inventories, fixed assets (land, buildings, machinery), and make investments.

  ⇨   Cash is reduced and other assets are increased.

➜   Any change in assets or liabilities or shareholders' equity is accompanied by an offsetting change that keeps the balance sheet in balance.

DOUBLE-ENTRY ACCOUNTING

➔ Double-entry accounting is an accounting system which records the two perspectives of every economic event:
- ⇨ Its source – where did funds come from?
- ⇨ Its use – how were the funds used?

➔ Every transaction is recorded through the use of a "credit" and an offsetting "debit" such that total debits always equal total credits in value.

- ⇨ Debits always represent uses of funds

- ⇨ Credits always represent sources of funds

➔ Double-entry accounting is depicted through the use of a "T account" (named for its resemblance to the letter T) in analyzing transactions:

T – Account Title

Debit (Dr.)	Credit (Cr.)
⇧ Increases in assets are depicted as debits	⇧ Increases in liabilities and shareholders' equity are depicted as credits
⇩ Decreases in liabilities and shareholders' equity are depicted as debits	⇩ Decreases in assets are depicted as credits

DOUBLE-ENTRY ACCOUNTING

➜ The balance sheet identity (A = L + E) can now be rewritten in a form of a T account:

Assets		=	Liabilities		+	Shareholders' Equity	
Debit (+)	Credit (-)		Debit (-)	Credit (+)		Debit (-)	Credit (+)

➜ Notice that debit and credit signs are reversed on the two sides of the balance sheet. Why?

⇨ Recall that debits always represent uses of funds

⇨ Credits always represent sources of funds

⇨ Uses of funds must always equal the sources of funds (Debits = Credits)

⇨ In the lemonade stand example, the increase in liabilities and shareholders' equity was a source of funds and thus a credit, offset fully by the corresponding rise in cash, representing a use of those funds and therefore a debit.

Exercise: Double-Entry Accounting

⇨ How would you illustrate the lemonade stand transaction, involving a bank loan of $50 and a $100 injection of your own money using T-accounts?

DOUBLE-ENTRY ACCOUNTING

Solution: Double-Entry Accounting

⇨   In this transaction, the bank loan and your own money are the two sources of funds and the cash raised represents the use of those funds.

⇨   Total debits (cash increase of $150) is equal to total credits (loan and own money amounting to $150).

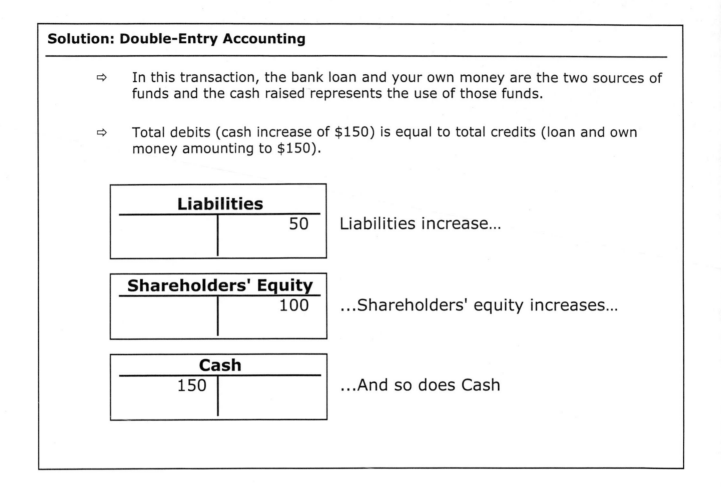

Liabilities

| | 50 |

Liabilities increase...

Shareholders' Equity

| | 100 |

...Shareholders' equity increases...

Cash

| 150 | |

...And so does Cash

DOUBLE-ENTRY ACCOUNTING

➔ Let's further expand the lemonade stand. After obtaining a $50 bank loan and putting up your own $100, you purchased $20 worth of lemons and paper cups as well as a lemon squeezer and lemonade stand for $30.

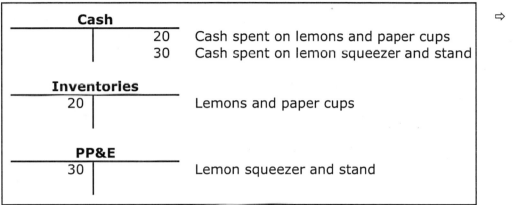

Cash		
	20	Cash spent on lemons and paper cups
	30	Cash spent on lemon squeezer and stand
Inventories		
20		Lemons and paper cups
PP&E		
30		Lemon squeezer and stand

⇨ In this transaction, cash is a source of funds (a credit) used to purchase inventories and PP&E, which were uses of those funds (debits)

Keep in mind:

➔ These transactions involved only assets; liabilities (bank loan of $50) and shareholders' equity ($100) did not change.

➔ At the inception of the lemonade stand, cash was a use of funds (debit), whereas it became a source of funds (credit) involving the purchase of inventories and fixed assets.

DOUBLE-ENTRY ACCOUNTING

➔ A modified method of recording the two purchases (on the previous slide) using double-entry accounting without the explicit use of the T account schematic is as follows:

	Debits (Dr.)	Credits (Cr.)
Inventories	20	
PP&E	30	
Cash		50

Why is double-entry accounting important?

➔ It facilitates understanding of the relationship between assets (resources) and liabilities/shareholders' equity (funding) of a company.

➔ The income statement, the balance sheet, and the statement of cash flows are connected; the relationship among these three statements and their impact on one another can often be initially "illustrated" through debits and credits.

Let's review the lemonade stand balance sheet at its inception – January 1, 2004

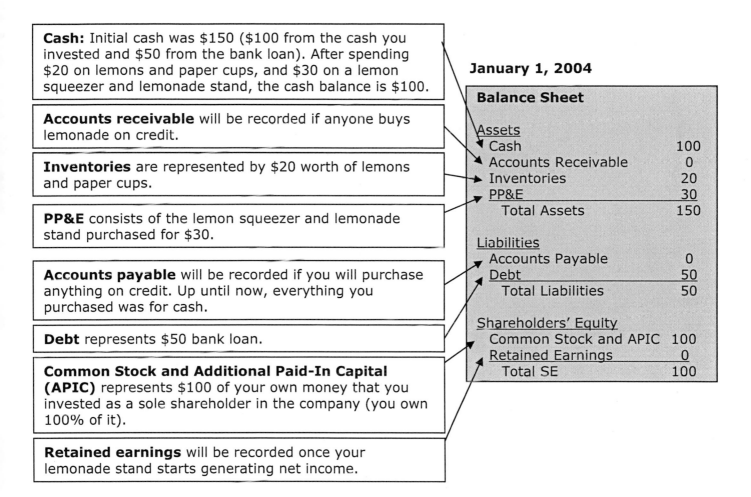

Cash: Initial cash was $150 ($100 from the cash you invested and $50 from the bank loan). After spending $20 on lemons and paper cups, and $30 on a lemon squeezer and lemonade stand, the cash balance is $100.

Accounts receivable will be recorded if anyone buys lemonade on credit.

Inventories are represented by $20 worth of lemons and paper cups.

PP&E consists of the lemon squeezer and lemonade stand purchased for $30.

Accounts payable will be recorded if you will purchase anything on credit. Up until now, everything you purchased was for cash.

Debt represents $50 bank loan.

Common Stock and Additional Paid-In Capital (APIC) represents $100 of your own money that you invested as a sole shareholder in the company (you own 100% of it).

Retained earnings will be recorded once your lemonade stand starts generating net income.

January 1, 2004

Balance Sheet

Assets	
Cash	100
Accounts Receivable	0
Inventories	20
PP&E	30
Total Assets	150

Liabilities	
Accounts Payable	0
Debt	50
Total Liabilities	50

Shareholders' Equity	
Common Stock and APIC	100
Retained Earnings	0
Total SE	100

INCOME STATEMENT REVISITED: LINKS TO BALANCE SHEET

➜ Recall the income statement for the lemonade stand that we developed earlier spanned January 1 – December 31, 2004 and generated $30m in net income:

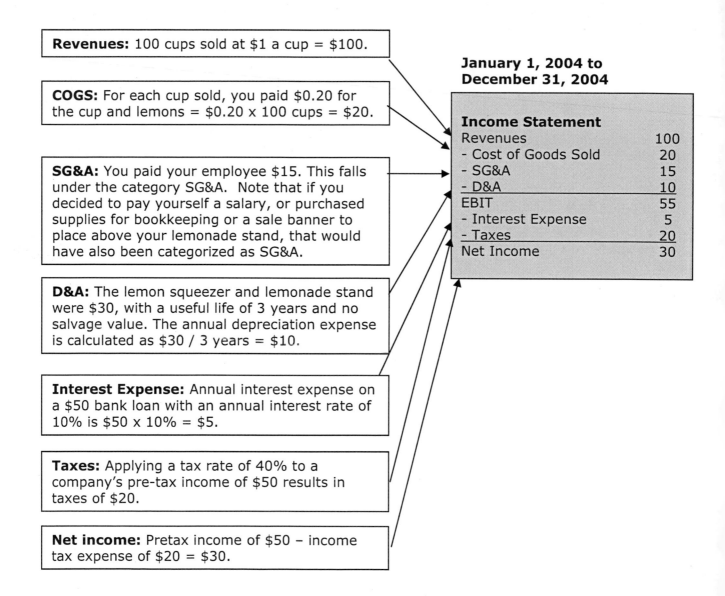

Revenues: 100 cups sold at $1 a cup = $100.

COGS: For each cup sold, you paid $0.20 for the cup and lemons = $0.20 x 100 cups = $20.

SG&A: You paid your employee $15. This falls under the category SG&A. Note that if you decided to pay yourself a salary, or purchased supplies for bookkeeping or a sale banner to place above your lemonade stand, that would have also been categorized as SG&A.

D&A: The lemon squeezer and lemonade stand were $30, with a useful life of 3 years and no salvage value. The annual depreciation expense is calculated as $30 / 3 years = $10.

Interest Expense: Annual interest expense on a $50 bank loan with an annual interest rate of 10% is $50 x 10% = $5.

Taxes: Applying a tax rate of 40% to a company's pre-tax income of $50 results in taxes of $20.

Net income: Pretax income of $50 – income tax expense of $20 = $30.

January 1, 2004 to December 31, 2004

Income Statement	
Revenues	100
- Cost of Goods Sold	20
- SG&A	15
- D&A	10
EBIT	55
- Interest Expense	5
- Taxes	20
Net Income	30

INCOME STATEMENT REVISITED: LINKS TO THE BALANCE SHEET

How is the balance sheet affected by the lemonade stand's profitability during the course of 2004?

➔ The income statement is connected to the balance sheet through retained earnings in shareholders' equity

⇨ Income (revenues, etc.) increases retained earnings
⇨ reflected as a credit to retained earnings

⇨ Expenses (COGS, SG&A, etc.) decrease retained earnings
⇨ reflected as debits to retained earnings

Income Statement

Retained Earnings

Assets		=	Liabilities		+	Shareholders' Equity	
Debit (+)	Credit (-)		Debit (-)	Credit (+)		Debit (-)	Credit (+)

Expenses (COGS, SG&A, etc.) are reflected as debits to retained earnings

Income (revenues, interest income, etc.) is reflected as a credit to retained earnings

INCOME STATEMENT REVISITED: LINKS TO THE BALANCE SHEET

Impact of Revenues on the Balance Sheet

➔ Your company generated $100 in revenues during the year (assume all cash), so increase your cash balance within the asset side of the balance sheet. The additional cash also increases your retained earnings within the shareholders' equity section.

Revenues ↑

Cash ↑

	Debits	Credits
Cash (A):	$100	
Revenues (SE):		$100

Impact of COGS on the Balance Sheet

➔ You recorded $20 worth of paper cups and lemons under inventories. These inventories were fully used up during the year (recall that the company also recorded $20 in COGS during the year).

➔ So inventories decreased by $20 to $0. Retained earnings were therefore reduced by $20.

COGS ↑

Inventories ↓

	Debits	Credits
COGS (SE):	$20	
Inventories (A):		$20

BALANCE SHEET

INCOME STATEMENT REVISITED: LINKS TO THE BALANCE SHEET

Impact of SG&A on the Balance Sheet

➜ You hired an employee and paid him $15 in cash. As a result, your cash balance was reduced by $15, and retained earnings were decreased by $15.

SG&A ↑

Cash ↓

	Debits	Credits
SG&A (SE):	$15	
Cash (A):		$15

Impact of Depreciation on the Balance Sheet

➜ Calculated depreciation of $10 was netted against existing fixed assets (property, plant & equipment), thereby reducing the PP&E balance from $30 to $20. Retained earnings were decreased by $10.

Depreciation ↑

Fixed Assets "PP&E" ↓

	Debits	Credits
Depreciation (SE):	$10	
PP&E (A):		$10

INCOME STATEMENT REVISITED: LINKS TO THE BALANCE SHEET

Impact of Interest Expense on the Balance Sheet

➜ During the year, you paid the bank the $5 interest expense on your loan.

➜ Accordingly, your cash balance was reduced along with the retained earnings account. Note that there was no impact on the debt balance because you have not paid down any principal.

Interest Expense ↑

Cash ↓

	Debits	Credits
Interest Expense (SE):	$5	
Cash (A):		$5

Impact of Tax Expense on the Balance Sheet

➜ Your cash balance was reduced by $20 when you paid your taxes, and the retained earnings account was also decreased by $20.

Tax Expense ↑

Cash ↓

	Debits	Credits
Tax Expense (SE):	$20	
Cash (A):		$20

INCOME STATEMENT REVISITED: LINKS TO THE BALANCE SHEET

Total impact of the year on the balance sheet:

Assets	Liabilities and SE
Cash	Retained Earnings
+$100 (Step 1)	+$100 (Step 1)
- $15 (Step 3)	-$20 (Step 2)
- $5 (Step 5)	-$15 (Step 3)
- $20 (Step 6)	-$10 (Step 4)
+60	-$5 (Step 5)
Inventories	-$20 (Step 6)
-$20 (Step 2)	**+30**
PP&E	
-$10 (Step 4)	

January 1, 2004

Balance Sheet	
Assets	
Cash	100
Accounts Receivable	0
Inventories	20
PP&E	30
Total Assets	150
Liabilities	
Accounts Payable	0
Debt	50
Total Liabilities	50
Shareholders' Equity	
Common Stock and APIC	100
Retained Earnings	0
Total SE	100

December 31, 2004

Balance Sheet		
Assets		
Cash	(+60)	160
Accounts Receivable	(no change)	0
Inventories	(-20)	0
PP&E	(-10)	20
Total Assets	(+30)	180
Liabilities		
Accounts Payable	(no change)	0
Debt	(no change)	50
Total Liabilities	(no change)	50
Shareholders' Equity		
Common Stock & APIC	(no change)	100
Retained Earnings	(+30)	30
Total SE	(+30)	130

INCOME STATEMENT REVISITED: LINKS TO THE BALANCE SHEET

January 1, 2004

Balance Sheet	
Assets	
Cash	100
Accounts Receivable	0
Inventories	20
PP&E	30
Total Assets	150
Liabilities	
Accounts Payable	0
Debt	50
Total Liabilities	50
Shareholders' Equity	
Common Stock and APIC	100
Retained Earnings	0
Total SE	100

January 1, 2004 to December 31, 2004

Income Statement	
Revenues	100
- Cost of Goods Sold	20
- SG&A	15
- D&A	10
EBIT	55
- Interest Expense	5
- Taxes	20
Net Income	30

December 31, 2004

Balance Sheet	
Assets	
Cash	160
Accounts Receivable	0
Inventories	0
PP&E	20
Total Assets	180
Liabilities	
Accounts Payable	0
Debt	50
Total Liabilities	50
Shareholders' Equity	
Common Stock & APIC	100
Retained Earnings	30
Total SE	130

Summary Notes

1. Observe that Assets always equal Liabilities + Shareholders' Equity. Understand the intuition behind the accounting equation. If you don't quite get it, go through this exercise again.

2. Also notice that retained earnings increased by $30 – that represents the $30 in net income that was generated during the year. Remember that the retained earnings account is the link between the balance sheet and the income statement.

ORDER OF LIQUIDITY

The balance sheet is organized in the descending order of liquidity

Assets

Liquidity ↓

⇨ Cash

⇨ Accounts receivable

⇨ Inventories

⇨ Fixed assets

⇨ Intangibles

Liabilities

When paid ↓

⇨ Accounts payable

⇨ Notes payable

⇨ Current portion of long-term debt

⇨ Long-term debt

⇨ Deferred income taxes

Microsoft 2004 Balance Sheet

(In millions) June 30	2003	2004
Assets		
Current assets:		
Cash and equivalents	$ 6,438	$ 15,982
Short-term investments	42,610	44,610
Total cash and short-term investments	49,048	60,592
Accounts receivable, net	5,196	5,890
Inventories	640	421
Deferred income taxes	2,506	2,097
Other	1,583	1,566
Total current assets	58,973	70,566
Property and equipment, net	2,223	2,326
Equity and other investments	13,692	12,210
Goodwill	3,128	3,115
Intangible assets, net	384	569
Deferred income taxes	2,161	1,829
Other long-term assets	1,171	1,774
Total assets	$ 81,732	$ 92,389
Liabilities and stockholders' equity		
Current liabilities:		
Accounts payable	$ 1,573	$ 1,717
Accrued compensation	1,416	1,339
Income taxes	2,044	3,478
Short-term unearned revenue	7,225	6,514
Other	1,716	1,921
Total current liabilities	13,974	14,969
Long-term unearned revenue	1,790	1,663
Other long-term liabilities	1,056	932
Commitments and contingencies		
Stockholders' equity:		
Common stock and paid-in capital – shares authorized 24,000; outstanding 10,771 and 10,862	49,234	56,396
Retained earnings, including accumulated other comprehensive income of $1,840 and $1,119	15,678	18,429
Total stockholders' equity	64,912	74,825
Total liabilities and stockholders' equity	$ 81,732	$ 92,389

ORDER OF LIQUIDITY

Current vs. Non-Current Assets

→ Current assets (such as merchandise in a store) are expected to be converted into cash within 12 months.

→ Non-current assets (such as a company's factories) are not expected to be converted into cash during the company's normal course of operations.

Current vs. Long-Term Liabilities

→ Current liabilities are to be paid within 12 months.

→ Long term liabilities (such as long-term debt) are not due within the year.

Microsoft 2004 Balance Sheet

(In millions) June 30	2003 [a]	2004
Assets		
Current assets:		
Cash and equivalents	$ 6,438	$ 15,982
Short-term investments	42,610	44,610
Total cash and short-term investments	49,048	60,592
Accounts receivable, net	5,196	5,890
Inventories	640	421
Deferred income taxes	2,506	2,097
Other	1,583	1,566
Total current assets	58,973	70,566
Property and equipment, net	2,223	2,326
Equity and other investments	13,692	12,210
Goodwill	3,128	3,115
Intangible assets, net	384	569
Deferred income taxes	2,161	1,829
Other long-term assets	1,171	1,774
Total assets	$ 81,732	$ 92,389
Liabilities and stockholders' equity		
Current liabilities:		
Accounts payable	$ 1,573	$ 1,717
Accrued compensation	1,416	1,339
Income taxes	2,044	3,478
Short-term unearned revenue	7,225	6,514
Other	1,716	1,921
Total current liabilities	13,974	14,969
Long-term unearned revenue	1,790	1,663
Other long-term liabilities	1,056	932
Commitments and contingencies		
Stockholders' equity:		
Common stock and paid-in capital – shares authorized 24,000; outstanding 10,771 and 10,862	49,234	56,396
Retained earnings, including accumulated other comprehensive income of $1,840 and $1,119	15,678	18,429
Total stockholders' equity	64,912	74,825
Total liabilities and stockholders' equity	$ 81,732	$ 92,389

Label each items as either:
⇨ Current asset
⇨ Non-current asset
⇨ Current liability
⇨ Long-term liability

1. Cash

2. Money owed to suppliers within 30 days

3. Six-month bank loan

4. Warehouse

5. Inventories waiting to be sold

6. A company's investment in another company

7. A 5-year bank loan

8. Employee salaries

9. Corporate jet

10. Which asset above is the most liquid? Why?

Label each items as either:
⇨ Current asset
⇨ Non-current asset
⇨ Current liability
⇨ Long-term liability

1. Cash

   CA

2. Money owed to suppliers within 30 days

   CL

3. Six-month bank loan

   CL

4. Warehouse

   NCA

5. Inventories waiting to be sold

   CA

6. A company's investment in another company

   CA or NCA

7. A 5-year bank loan

   LTL

8. Employee salaries

   CL

9. Corporate jet

   NCA

10. Which asset above is the most liquid? Why?

   Cash is the most liquid asset – it's already cash!

ASSETS

Cash is money held by the company in its bank accounts.

Cash equivalents are extremely liquid assets; examples include U.S. Treasury bills, which have a term of less than or equal to 90 days.

Marketable securities (short-term investments) are debt or equity securities held by the company.

Microsoft 2004 Balance Sheet

(In millions) June 30		2003 (9)	2004
Assets			
Current assets:			
Cash and equivalents	$	6,438	$ 15,982
Short-term investments		42,610	44,610
Total cash and short-term investments		49,048	60,592
Accounts receivable, net		5,196	5,890
Inventories		640	421
Deferred income taxes		2,506	2,097
Other		1,583	1,566
Total current assets		58,973	70,566
Property and equipment, net		2,223	2,326
Equity and other investments		13,692	12,210
Goodwill		3,128	3,115
Intangible assets, net		384	569
Deferred income taxes		2,161	1,829
Other long-term assets		1,171	1,774
Total assets	$	81,732	$ 92,389

⇨ Treasury bills, money market funds, notes, bonds, and equity securities.

→ Different companies may categorize their liquid holdings as either cash equivalents or marketable securities.

→ Both are considered very liquid (i.e. easily convertible into cash).

ASSETS

Accounts Receivable represent sales that a company has made on credit; the product has been sold and delivered, but the company has not yet received the cash for the sale.

Accounts receivable are typically abbreviated as AR.

Microsoft 2004 Balance Sheet

(In millions) June 30		2003	2004
Assets			
Current assets:			
Cash and equivalents	$	6,438	$ 15,982
Short-term investments		42,610	44,610
Total cash and short-term investments		49,048	60,592
Accounts receivable, net		5,196	5,890
Inventories		640	421
Deferred income taxes		2,506	2,097
Other		1,583	1,566
Total current assets		58,973	70,566
Property and equipment, net		2,223	2,326
Equity and other investments		13,692	12,210
Goodwill		3,128	3,115
Intangible assets, net		384	569
Deferred income taxes		2,161	1,829
Other long-term assets		1,171	1,774
Total assets	$	81,732	$ 92,389

Accounts receivable are linked to Revenues on the income statement:

→ Suppose customers buy $1000 worth of items on credit:

	Dr.	Cr.
AR (A)	1000	
Revenues (SE)		1000

→ Now what if customers end up paying $800 but don't pay the rest?

→ Net revenues are then $1000 - $200

	Dr.	Cr.
Cash (A)	800	
Returns (SE)	200	
AR (A)		1000

Exercise: The Lemonade Stand

⇨ Recall that during 2004, the lemonade stand recorded revenues of $100 on its income statement.

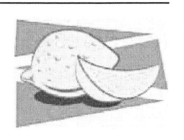

⇨ We previously assumed that the company collected the entire revenue amount in cash.

⇨ Now assume the following:

1. It collected $50 in cash and $50 on credit.

2. 5% of the credit purchases were returned, and the rest were eventually collected.

Based on the new information:

1. Create the appropriate T-account for each transaction

2. Calculate net revenues

Solution: The Lemonade Stand

Transaction 1: It collected $50 in cash and $50 on credit:

	Dr.	Cr.
Cash (A)	50	
AR (A)	50	
Revenues (SE)		100

Revenues ↑

Cash ↑
AR ↑

Transaction 2: 5% of the credit purchases were returned, the rest were eventually collected:

	Dr.	Cr.
Cash (A)	47.5	
Revenues (SE)	2.5	
AR (A)		50

Net revenues = $97.5

BALANCE SHEET

ASSETS

Inventories represent goods waiting to be sold, and direct and (sometimes indirect) costs associated with the production or procurement of these goods.

The composition of inventories depends on the nature of a company's business; they typically consist of three major categories:

Microsoft 2004 Balance Sheet

(In millions) June 30	2003	2004
Assets		
Current assets:		
Cash and equivalents	$ 6,438	$ 15,982
Short-term investments	42,610	44,610
Total cash and short-term investments	49,048	60,592
Accounts receivable, net	5,196	5,890
Inventories	640	421
Deferred income taxes	2,506	2,097
Other	1,583	1,566
Total current assets	58,973	70,566
Property and equipment, net	2,223	2,326
Equity and other investments	13,692	12,210
Goodwill	3,128	3,115
Intangible assets, net	384	569
Deferred income taxes	2,161	1,829
Other long-term assets	1,171	1,774
Total assets	$ 81,732	$ 92,389

1. **Raw materials**: Used in the manufacture of the finished product such as crude oil, food products.

2. **Work-in-process**: Products in the process of being manufactured such as cars/computers in the middle of assembly.

3. **Finished goods**: Products that have been completed and are ready for sale such as clothes, books, cars.

Inventories are linked to COGS on the income statement:

→ Suppose a company sells $50 worth of inventories during the year:

	Dr.	Cr.
COGS (SE)	50	
Inventories (A)		50

ASSETS

Inventories are linked to the COGS line of the income statement:

➜   Recall that Cost of Goods Sold (COGS) refers to the direct cost of buying raw materials and converting them into finished products or services.

➜   Before these costs become part of COGS (on the income statement) and are matched to the revenues they help generate (under the matching principle of accrual accounting), they are part of the company's inventories (on the balance sheet), such that:

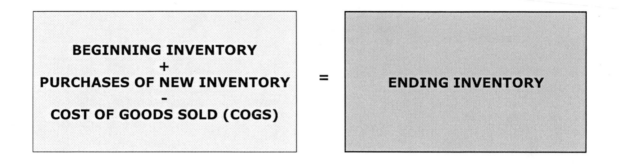

| BEGINNING INVENTORY
+
PURCHASES OF NEW INVENTORY
-
COST OF GOODS SOLD (COGS) | = | ENDING INVENTORY |

Exercise: Inventories

Your firm sells office supplies:

⇨   Beginning inventories = $500,000
⇨   COGS during period = $200,000
⇨   New inventories purchased = $300,000

Calculate ending inventory balance

Solution: Inventories

⇨ Your firm sells office supplies:
⇨ Beginning inventories = $500,000
⇨ COGS during period = $200,000
⇨ New inventories purchased = $300,000

Calculate ending inventory balance:

| BEGINNING INVENTORY
+
PURCHASES OF NEW INVENTORY
-
COST OF GOODS SOLD (COGS)
=
ENDING INVENTORY | = | $500,000
+
$300,000
-
$200,000
=
$600,000 |

BALANCE SHEET

ASSETS

Problem: Cost of office supplies changes – you bought a stapler for $2 that has been sitting in inventories; 6 months later you buy a stapler for your inventories for $2.50.

What value do we assign to COGS, and what value should ending inventories hold?

Three different methods of inventory accounting have been established to answer this question.

1. **First In, First Out (FIFO)**
   - ⇨ The items first purchased (first in) are the first to be sold (COGS – first out). Therefore, the cost of inventory first acquired (beginning inventory – first in) is assigned to COGS (first out). Ending inventory reflects the cost of the most recently purchased inventories.

2. **Last In, First Out (LIFO)**
   - ⇨ The items purchased last (last in) are the first to be sold (COGS – first out). Therefore, the cost of inventory most recently acquired (ending inventory – last in) is assigned to COGS (first out). Ending inventory reflects the cost of the first purchased inventories.

3. **Average Cost**
   - ⇨ COGS and ending inventory are calculated as COGS divided by total number of goods.

Exercise: Inventories

⇨ Your firm sells staplers:

Inventory Purchases	Sales
50 units at $2	20 units at $4
20 units at $3	30 units at $5
30 units at $4	17 units at $7

⇨ Beginning Inventories = 35 units at $1

⇨ Calculate ending inventory balance
- Under FIFO
- Under LIFO
- Under Average Cost

⇨ Calculate gross profit
- Under FIFO
- Under LIFO
- Under Average Cost

Solution: Inventories

LIFO		FIFO		Average Cost	
Sales		**Sales**		**Sales**	
Units	Sales	Units	Sales	Units	Sales
20	$80	20	$80	20	$80
30	$150	30	$150	30	$150
17	$119	17	$119	17	$119
67	$349	67	$349	67	$349
COGS		**COGS**		**COGS**	
Units	Cost	Units	Cost	Units	Cost
30	$120	35	$35	67	$156
20	$60	32	$64		
17	$34				
67	$214	67	$99	67	$156
Gross Margin		**Gross Margin**		**Gross Margin**	
	$135		$250		$193
Inventories		**Inventories**		**Inventories**	
Units	Cost	Units	Cost	Units	Cost
35	$35	18	$36	68	$159
33	$66	20	$60		
		30	$120		
68	$101	68	$216	68	$159

LIFO Reserve = FIFO Inv - LIFO Inv. = $115

Highlights

Because our example assumed that the prices of inventories were rising, note how reported COGS were higher using LIFO vs. FIFO

⇨ This implies lower net income under LIFO and thus lower taxes.

⇨ The tax benefit of LIFO accounting is what makes it preferable for many U.S. companies over FIFO accounting in periods of rising inventory prices.

⇨ Note that LIFO accounting is not allowed in Europe.

LIFO Reserve – The Link between FIFO and LIFO Inventory Methods

➔ When companies use the LIFO method, their footnotes must disclose what the value of their inventories would be under the FIFO method. The LIFO Reserve is used to convert the value of inventories between the two methods, such that:

LIFO Reserve = Inventory (FIFO Basis) – Inventory (LIFO Basis)

➔ **Application**: When comparing a company that accounts for inventories using LIFO with a company using FIFO, the LIFO reserve must be added to the LIFO company's inventory levels to arrive at FIFO inventory levels for an apples-to-apples comparison.

BALANCE SHEET

ASSETS

Writing down inventories

➜ Recall that the balance sheet shows assets – including inventories – at their historical (acquisition) cost – in conjunction with the historical cost principle.

➜ Inventories may deteriorate physically or become obsolete, causing their value to fall. What happens when the value of inventories falls below their historical cost?

➜ Lower of cost-or-market (LCM) rule dictates that if the market value (or replacement cost) of inventories falls below their historical cost, they must be written down to this lower market value, and the loss must be recognized immediately.

> **Inventory Write-Down = Historical Cost (Book Value) – Market Value**

⇨ The LCM rule is an example of the conservatism principle.

⇨ Unlike inventory losses, inventory gains can only be recognized when that inventory is sold.

➜ Recalling our lemonade stand example, suppose that lemons sitting in inventories rot and are determined to be un-sellable; a $5 write-down has to take place. Here is how it affects the financial statements:

	Dr.	Cr.
COGS (SE)[1]	5	
Inventories (A)		5

---

[1] Sometimes companies disclose large write-downs separately on the income statement; other times they include them in COGS.

ASSETS

Deferred tax assets

→ See a detailed discussion of deferred taxes on page 181.

Other current assets is a "catch-all" category that includes miscellaneous current assets, such as:

→ Short-term investments

→ Pre-paid expenses

Microsoft 2004 Balance Sheet

(In millions) June 30	2003	2004
Assets		
Current assets:		
Cash and equivalents	$ 6,438	$ 15,982
Short-term investments	42,610	44,610
Total cash and short-term investments	49,048	60,592
Accounts receivable, net	5,196	5,890
Inventories	640	421
Deferred income taxes	2,506	2,097
Other	1,583	1,566
Total current assets	58,973	70,566
Property and equipment, net	2,223	2,326
Equity and other investments	13,692	12,210
Goodwill	3,128	3,115
Intangible assets, net	384	569
Deferred income taxes	2,161	1,829
Other long-term assets	1,171	1,774
Total assets	$ 81,732	$ 92,389

⇨ Represent operating expenses that have been pre-paid by the company in advance for services it is yet to receive.

⇨ Consist of:
- Insurance premiums
- Property rents
- Salary advances

ASSETS

Property, Plant & Equipment (PPE) represent land, buildings, and machinery used in the manufacture of the company's services and products plus all costs (transportation, installation, other) necessary to prepare those fixed assets for their service.

PP&E is linked to depreciation on the income statement

Recall that depreciation is the systematic allocation of the cost of fixed assets over their estimated useful lives; PP&E represent those fixed assets.

PP&E is also referred to as:
⇨ Fixed Assets
⇨ Tangible Assets

Suppose depreciation expense in Year 1 is $100. Its effect on the balance sheet (a decrease in PP&E) can be illustrated through credits and debits:

Microsoft 2004 Balance Sheet

(In millions) June 30		2003	2004
Assets			
Current assets:			
Cash and equivalents	$	6,438	$ 15,982
Short-term investments		42,610	44,610
Total cash and short-term investments		49,048	60,592
Accounts receivable, net		5,196	5,890
Inventories		640	421
Deferred income taxes		2,506	2,097
Other		1,583	1,566
Total current assets		58,973	70,566
Property and equipment, net		2,223	2,326
Equity and other investments		13,692	12,210
Goodwill		3,128	3,115
Intangible assets, net		384	569
Deferred income taxes		2,161	1,829
Other long-term assets		1,171	1,774
Total assets	$	81,732	$ 92,389

	Dr.	Cr.
Depreciation Expense (SE)	100	
PP&E (A)		100

ASSETS

PP&E, net of depreciation

PP&E is reported net of accumulated depreciation on the balance sheet, such that:

$$\textbf{Net PP\&E = Gross PP\&E - Accumulated Depreciation}$$

Accumulated depreciation = sum of all depreciation expenses (net of asset sales) on the income statement.

→ It is a contra account, which is an offsetting account to an asset (and can also be to liabilities and shareholders' equity).

⇨ Increases in a contra account reduce the associated asset account

→ Accumulated depreciation offsets Gross PP&E account, and the 2 accounts are aggregated together on the balance sheet as Net PP&E.

Accumulated Depreciation (B/S) =
$(\text{Depreciation Expense})_{\text{Year 1}}$
$+ (\text{Depreciation Expense})_{\text{Year 2}}$
$+ (\text{Depreciation Expense})_{\text{Year 3}}$
$+ \ldots$
$+ (\text{Depreciation Expense})_{\text{Current Year}}$

ASSETS

Reconciliation of PP&E

Additions to PP&E

PP&E
Beginning of
Year

Capital
Expenditures
During the Year

PP&E
End of year

Depreciation
Expense
During the Year

Asset Sales/
Write-Offs
During the Year

Reduction to PP&E

Exercise: The Lemonade Stand

⇨ Recall that on January 1, 2004, you bought a lemon squeezer and a lemonade stand for $30. You estimate that both of these fixed assets will have a useful life of 3 years, upon which they will be obsolete and be thrown away (assume straight-line depreciation).

⇨ Calculate PP&E at the end of 2004, 2005, and 2006

January 1, 2004

Balance Sheet

Assets
Cash	100
Accounts Receivable	0
Inventories	20
PP&E	30
Total Assets	150

Liabilities
Accounts Payable	0
Debt	50
Total Liabilities	50

Shareholders' Equity
Common Stock and APIC	100
Retained Earnings	0
Total SE	100

January 1, 2004 to December 31, 2004

Income Statement
Revenues	100
- Cost of Goods Sold	20
- SG&A	15
- D&A	10
EBIT	55
- Interest Expense	5
- Taxes	20
Net Income	30

December 31, 2004

Balance Sheet

Assets
Cash	160
Accounts Receivable	0
Inventories	0
PP&E	20
Total Assets	180

Liabilities
Accounts Payable	0
Debt	50
Total Liabilities	50

Shareholders' Equity
Common Stock & APIC	100
Retained Earnings	30
Total SE	130

Solution: The Lemonade Stand

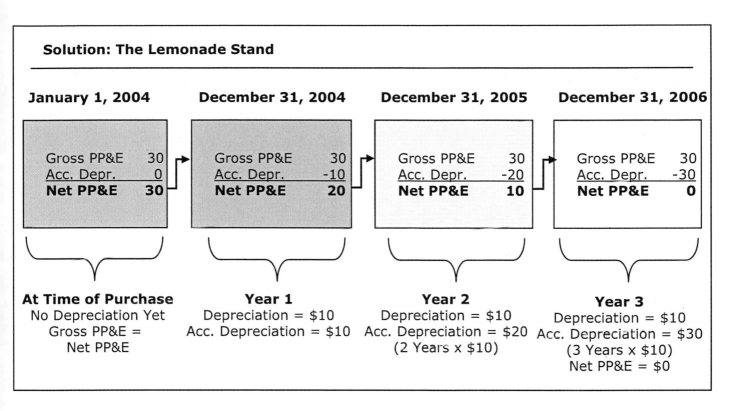

January 1, 2004

Gross PP&E	30
Acc. Depr.	0
Net PP&E	**30**

December 31, 2004

Gross PP&E	30
Acc. Depr.	-10
Net PP&E	**20**

December 31, 2005

Gross PP&E	30
Acc. Depr.	-20
Net PP&E	**10**

December 31, 2006

Gross PP&E	30
Acc. Depr.	-30
Net PP&E	**0**

At Time of Purchase
No Depreciation Yet
Gross PP&E =
Net PP&E

Year 1
Depreciation = $10
Acc. Depreciation = $10

Year 2
Depreciation = $10
Acc. Depreciation = $20
(2 Years x $10)

Year 3
Depreciation = $10
Acc. Depreciation = $30
(3 Years x $10)
Net PP&E = $0

Exercise: PP&E

A company has PP&E of $4,000 in January 1, 2004

- ⇨ It records depreciation of $800 during 2004
- ⇨ It buys 5 new machines for $500 during 2004
- ⇨ It sells 2 old machines for $100 during 2004

Calculate PP&E at December 31, 2004

Solution: PP&E

Beginning PP&E	= $4,000
- Depreciation	= -$800
+ New machines purchased	= +$500
- Old machines sold	= -$100
Ending PP&E	= $3,600

ASSETS

Capitalizing Vs. Expensing

➔ Capitalizing involves the recording of costs/expenditures associated with fixed assets on the balance sheet and their depreciation (on the income statement) over their estimated useful lives.

➔ Expensing involves the immediate recording of costs/expenditures on the income statement.

➔ Fixed assets (acquired or self-constructed) are capitalized and depreciated along with costs necessary to prepare those fixed assets for their service. These costs include:

⇨ Transportation charges
⇨ Freight & insurance costs
⇨ Installation
⇨ Other (sales tax)
⇨ Fixed asset labor
⇨ Materials
⇨ Interest on debt borrowed in connection with that asset

Should costs subsequent to fixed asset acquisition or construction be capitalized or expensed?

➔ General guidelines dictate that costs incurred to achieve greater future benefits from fixed assets should be capitalized. Greater benefits may be in the form of:

⇨ Increased quality or quantity or extended useful life of an asset

⇨ Improvements to fixed assets

⇨ Since these costs raise the future benefits expected from those assets, they should therefore be capitalized and depreciated

Expenditures that simply maintain the same level of operations should be expensed

➔ Repairs & maintenance generally involve restoring an asset to and maintaining its operating condition, and are therefore immediately expensed.

ASSETS

Fixed Asset Impairments

➜ Fixed assets can become impaired if their book value (i.e. historical costs) is likely not to be recovered during their future operations.

➜ Multiple events can cause impairments of fixed assets to occur:

 ⇨ A substantial decline in market value, physical change, or usage of fixed assets

 ⇨ Significant legal or business climate change

 ⇨ Excessive costs associated with their operations

 ⇨ Expected operating losses or lower than expected profitability stemming from these assets

➜ The conservatism principle dictates that once an asset has been written down (the lowered fair market value will become the new book value), it cannot be written up in the future.

FASB 121 established a two-step process to determine if impairment has occurred:

 1. A Recoverability Test

 ⇨ Impairment has taken place if an asset's book value exceeds the undiscounted cash flows expected from its use *and* disposal.

 2. Loss Measurement

 ⇨ If impairment occurs, the book value of a fixed asset has to be written down to its lowered fair market value on the balance sheet:

$$\text{Impairment Amount} = \text{Book Value} - \text{Fair Market Value}$$

The loss associated with the write-down of an asset on the balance sheet must also be shown on the income statement as part of unusual or infrequent item category (recall nonrecurring items!)

 ➜ Remember: since the value of a fixed asset is reduced, a corresponding decrease must occur on the liabilities & shareholders' equity side.

ASSETS

Fixed Asset Retirement and Disposal

Companies often remove fixed assets from service when those assets become obsolete because of physical (deterioration) or economic (technological innovation) factors.

Assets can also be sold (disposed of) through their sale to another company.

➜ The remaining gross PP&E and accumulated depreciation of a sold asset are removed from the balance sheet.

➜ "Gain/loss on disposal of an asset" is recorded pre-tax on the income statement.

⇨ Recall that gain/loss on asset sales is considered part of nonrecurring items ("infrequent or unusual items" category).

Phase of Fixed Asset Life	Overview	Accounting Treatment
Acquired or Self-Constructed	Land, buildings, and machinery used in the manufacture of the company's services and products **plus** all costs necessary to prepare those fixed assets for their service	Capitalized (B/S) and depreciated (IS)
Repairs, Maintenance & Improvements	Services necessary to keep fixed assets operational	Repairs & Maintenance: Expensed (IS) Improvements: Capitalized (B/S) and depreciated (IS)
Impairment	An asset's book value exceeds the undiscounted cash flows expected from its use and disposal	Book value reduced (B/S); Loss associated with this write-down is expensed (IS)
Retirement & Disposal	Removal from service (possibly through sale)	Gross PP&E and accumulated depreciation associated with retired asset are removed; Gain/loss on disposal of assets (if sold) is recorded

BALANCE SHEET

ASSETS

Companies often make investments for various strategic reasons:

→ Partnerships and joint ventures

→ Investments in start-up technologies, new regions

In accounting, such investments can be broadly placed into three categories, depending on the percentage of ownership in them and the resulting level of control over them:

Microsoft 2004 Balance Sheet

(In millions) June 30		2003	2004
Assets			
Current assets:			
Cash and equivalents	$	6,438 $	16,982
Short-term investments		42,610	44,610
Total cash and short-term investments		49,048	60,592
Accounts receivable, net		5,196	5,890
Inventories		640	421
Deferred income taxes		2,506	2,097
Other		1,583	1,566
Total current assets		58,973	70,566
Property and equipment, net		2,223	2,326
Equity and other investments		13,692	12,210
Goodwill		3,128	3,115
Intangible assets, net		384	569
Deferred income taxes		2,161	1,829
Other long-term assets		1,171	1,774
Total assets	$	81,732 $	92,389

1. **Investments in Securities** (<20% ownership)
   ⇨ Level of Influence: None / Little
   ⇨ Reporting method: Cost or Market

2. **Equity Investments** (usually between 20%-50% ownership)
   ⇨ Level of Influence: Significant
   ⇨ Reporting method: Equity Method

3. **Consolidation** (usually >50% ownership)
   ⇨ Level of Influence: Control
   ⇨ Reporting method: Consolidation

BALANCE SHEET

ASSETS

1. Investments in Securities

➔ Such investments can take a form of equity or debt (marketable) securities.

➔ A general guideline is for a company to hold less than 20% ownership interest in another company.

➔ These investments are measured at their cost (acquisition price) if there is not a readily available market to determine fair market price.

➔ SFAS 115 requires publicly-traded securities to be recorded at their fair market value.
   ⇨ Notice that this is a deviation from the historical cost principle.

---

3 Major Categories of Security Investments:

---

1. **Debt securities held to maturity**
   ⇨ Recorded at their cost
2. **Securities available for sale**
   ⇨ Recorded at their fair market value
3. **Trading securities**
   ⇨ Recorded at their fair market value

What determines the classification of security investments?
   ⇨ Their classification depends largely on management intent

---

2. Equity Investments

➔ Such "strategic" investments can take a form of equity or debt securities.

➔ A general guideline is for a company to hold 20%-50% ownership interest in another company, thereby exercising a certain level of operational and strategic control.

➔ These investments are measured at their cost (acquisition price).

EMC Corp. 2004 10-K

[Investments in Securities]   [Equity Investments]

Investments

Our investments are comprised primarily of debt securities that are classified as available-for-sale and recorded at their fair market value. Investments with remaining maturities of less than twelve months from the balance sheet date are classified as short-term investments. Investments with remaining maturities of more than twelve months from the balance sheet date are classified as long-term investments.

We also hold strategic equity investments. Strategic equity investments in publicly traded companies are classified as available-for-sale when there are no restrictions on our ability to liquidate such securities. These investments are also carried at their market value. Strategic equity investments in privately-held companies are carried at the lower of cost or net realizable value due to their illiquid nature. We review these investments to ascertain whether unrealized losses are other than temporary.

Unrealized gains and temporary losses on investments classified as available-for-sale are included as a separate component of stockholders' equity, net of any related tax effect. Realized gains and losses and other-than-temporary impairments on non-strategic investments are reflected in the statement of operations in investment income. Realized gains and losses and other-than-temporary impairments on strategic investments are reflected in the statement of operations in other expense, net. Investment activity is accounted for using the average cost, first-in, first-out and specific lot methods.

ASSETS

3. Consolidation

➜ The consolidation method is used for majority-owned investments (greater than 50%) in another business entity to reflect the investing company's virtually complete operational and strategic control of the entity.

➜ The consolidation method calls for the consolidation of the financial reports of the parent company (assets, liabilities, shareholders' equity, revenues, net income, etc.) with all businesses in which it holds a greater than 50% ownership stake.

➜ Global corporations may have hundreds of such subsidiaries, which are often focused on specific geography, division, product line, or service.

ExxonMobil 2003 10-K

Consolidations

The consolidated financial statements include the accounts of those significant subsidiaries that the corporation controls. They also include the corporation's undivided interests in upstream assets and liabilities. Amounts representing the corporation's percentage interest in the underlying net assets of other significant affiliates that it does not control, but exercises significant influence, are included in "Investments and advances"; the corporation's share of the net income of these companies is included in the consolidated statement of income caption "Income from equity affiliates." The accounting for these non-consolidated companies is referred to as the equity method of accounting.

Majority ownership is normally the indicator of control that is the basis on which subsidiaries are consolidated. However, certain factors may indicate that a majority-owned investment is not controlled and therefore should be accounted for using the equity method of accounting. These factors occur where the minority shareholders are granted by law or by contract substantive participating rights. These include the right to approve operating policies, expense budgets, financing and investment plans and management compensation and succession plans.

ASSETS

Intangible assets are comprised of non-physical acquired assets and include:

- ⇨ Brand
- ⇨ Franchise
- ⇨ Trademarks
- ⇨ Patents
- ⇨ Customer Lists
- ⇨ Licenses
- ⇨ Goodwill

These intangible assets are items that have value based on the rights belonging to that company.

Microsoft 2004 Balance Sheet

(In millions) June 30		2003 (a)	2004
Assets			
Current assets:			
Cash and equivalents	$	6,438	$ 15,982
Short-term investments		42,610	44,610
Total cash and short-term investments		49,048	60,592
Accounts receivable, net		5,196	5,890
Inventories		640	421
Deferred income taxes		2,506	2,097
Other		1,583	1,566
Total current assets		58,973	70,566
Property and equipment, net		2,223	2,326
Equity and other investments		13,692	12,210
Goodwill		3,128	3,115
Intangible assets, net		384	569
Deferred income taxes		2,161	1,829
Other long-term assets		1,171	1,774
Total assets	$	81,732	$ 92,389

Intangible assets are only recognized when they are purchased (acquired)!

- ⤷ The value of internally-developed intangibles cannot be accurately quantified and recorded (think back to Coke, GE, Microsoft).

- ⤷ Companies are not permitted to assign values to these brand names, trademarks, etc. unless the value is readily observable in the market (via an acquisition).

BALANCE SHEET

ASSETS

Intangible assets are linked to amortization on the income statement

➜ Recall that amortization is the systematic allocation of intangible assets over an estimated useful life. Intangible assets are reduced on the balance sheet via amortization on the income statement.

➜ Intangible assets are amortized, just like fixed assets are depreciated, over their useful lives.

⇨ Suppose a drugstore acquired a pharmacy customer list from another drugstore 2 years ago for $100.

⇨ This customer list is recorded as an intangible asset on the balance sheet and amortized over 5 years at $20 per year.

⇨ This year, the impact on the financial statements would be as follows:

	Dr.	Cr.
Amortization Expense (SE)	20	
Intangible Assets (A)		20

ASSETS

Goodwill is the amount by which the purchase price for a company exceeds its fair market value (FMV), representing the "intangible" value stemming from the acquired company's business name, customer relations, employee morale.

It is important to remember that goodwill is created only after <u>all</u> identifiable physical and intangible assets (patents, licenses) have been assigned fair market value.

Microsoft 2004 Balance Sheet

(In millions)			
June 30		2003 (a)	2004
Assets			
Current assets:			
Cash and equivalents	$	6,438	$ 15,982
Short-term investments		42,610	44,610
Total cash and short-term investments		49,048	60,592
Accounts receivable, net		5,196	5,890
Inventories		640	421
Deferred income taxes		2,506	2,097
Other		1,583	1,566
Total current assets		58,973	70,566
Property and equipment, net		2,223	2,326
Equity and other investments		13,692	12,210
Goodwill		3,128	3,115
Intangible assets, net		384	569
Deferred income taxes		2,161	1,829
Other long-term assets		1,171	1,774
Total assets	$	81,732	$ 92,389

No longer amortized after 2001

Before December 15, 2001: goodwill on the balance sheet was amortized on the income statement under U.S. GAAP.

After December 15, 2001: Under a FASB ruling (SFAS 142), goodwill is no longer amortized on the income statement.

ASSETS

Annual Impairment Tests

The Boeing Company 2003 Balance Sheet

➔ Instead, the acquired assets that had generated goodwill need to be periodically (annually) tested for impairment (loss of value).

➔ If an asset is determined to be impaired, the goodwill is adjusted down to better reflect current market value (goodwill write-down).

CONSOLIDATED STATEMENTS OF FINANCIAL POSITION

(Dollars in millions except per share data)		2003		2002
December 31,				
Assets				
Cash and cash equivalents	$	4,633	$	2,333
Accounts receivable		4,515		5,007
Current portion of customer and commercial financing		857		1,289
Income taxes receivable		199		
Deferred income taxes		1,716		2,042
Inventories, net of advances, progress billings and reserves		5,338		6,184
Total current assets		17,258		16,855
Customer and commercial financing, net		12,094		10,922
Property, plant and equipment, net		8,432		8,765
Goodwill		1,913		2,760
Other acquired intangibles, net		1,035		1,128
Prepaid pension expense		8,542		6,671
Deferred income taxes		1,242		2,272
Other assets		2,519		2,969
	$	53,035	$	52,342

> **"We also recognized $913 million in goodwill charges as a result of a goodwill impairment analysis triggered by the reorganization of our Military Aircraft and Missile Systems and Space and Communications segments . . ."**
> **-- The Boeing Company (2003 10-K)**

➔ Write-downs are expensed through the income statement (non-cash expense as there is no real impact on cash) and imply that a company overpaid for an asset.

➔ Goodwill can only be written down, not up: if Big-Time Furniture determines that the asset (Johnny's Interiors) is worth more than the original purchase price, it cannot increase the amount of goodwill on its balance sheet, in-line with the conservatism principle.

Type of Intangible Asset	Overview	Accounting Treatment	Tax Treatment
Patent	Exclusive right from the federal government to sell a product or Process for a 17-year period	Amortization over useful life (up to 17 years)	Tax-deductible (income statement)
Copyright	A federally-granted right covering artistic materials during the creator's life plus 50 years	Amortization over useful life (not to exceed 40 years)	Tax-deductible (income statement)
Trademarks & Brand Names	A registered symbol or name reserved exclusively for its owner for an indefinite number of periods (renewed every 20 years)	Amortization over useful life (not to exceed 40 years)	Tax-deductible (income statement)
Leaseholds	A long-term rental contract for the right to occupy land or buildings	Amortization over useful life of the lease	Tax-deductible (income statement)
Franchises & Licenses	A right to an exclusive manufacture or sale of products or services	Amortization over useful life (not to exceed 40 years)	Tax-deductible (income statement)
Goodwill	The amount by which the purchase price for a company exceeds its fair market value (FMV)	No longer amortized after 12/15/01; Undergoes annual impairment test	NOT tax-deductible (income statement)

ASSETS

→ **Other assets** is a "catch-all" category that includes miscellaneous non-current assets, which are not considered fixed or intangible.

→ Such other assets may include pre-paid expenses and some types of long-term investments.

Microsoft 2004 Balance Sheet

(In millions) June 30		2003	2004
Assets			
Current assets:			
Cash and equivalents	$	6,438	$ 15,982
Short-term investments		42,610	44,610
Total cash and short-term investments		49,048	60,592
Accounts receivable, net		5,196	5,890
Inventories		640	421
Deferred income taxes		2,506	2,097
Other		1,583	1,566
Total current assets		58,973	70,566
Property and equipment, net		2,223	2,326
Equity and other investments		13,692	12,210
Goodwill		3,128	3,115
Intangible assets, net		384	569
Deferred income taxes		2,161	1,829
Other long-term assets		1,171	1,774
Total assets	$	81,732	$ 92,389

LIABILITIES

Liabilities represent the company's obligations to others

➜ To qualify as a liability, an obligation must be measurable and its occurrence probable

---

Liabilities typically consist of (but are not always limited to):

LIABILITIES

Accounts Payable	A company's obligations to suppliers for services and products already purchased from them, but which have not been paid. In other words, accounts payable represent the company's unpaid bills to its suppliers for services obtained on credit from them.
Notes Payable	Debt or equity securities held by the company
Current Portion of Long-Term Debt	Portion of debt with an overall maturity of more than a year; this portion is due within 12 months
Long-Term Debt	The company's borrowings with a maturity (full repayment) exceeding 12 months
Deferred Taxes	Potential future tax obligations arising when taxes payable to the IRS are lower than those recorded on financial statements
Minority Interest	Equity interest in the portion of the consolidated businesses that the company does not own

---

Liabilities represent obligations stemming from a company's:

1. Operating activities, and
2. Financing activities

Liabilities generally possess the following characteristics:

☑ They are obligations that will be met through the use of cash, goods, or services.
☑ The transactions from which these obligations arise have taken place.

On the balance sheet, liabilities are divided into 2 categories:

➜ Current liabilities

⇨ Due within 1 year
⇨ Reported in order of maturity, by amount, or in the event of liquidation

➜ Long-term liabilities

⇨ Obligations not due within a year

LIABILITIES

Accounts payable is a current liability representing amounts owed by the company to suppliers for prior purchases or services.

→ Suppose you purchased $7 of your lemons from a fruit supplier on credit, promising to pay him back in a month. Here is the impact on the financial statements:

Microsoft 2004 Balance Sheet

Liabilities and stockholders' equity			
Current liabilities:			
Accounts payable	$	1,573	$ 1,717
Accrued compensation		1,416	1,339
Income taxes		2,044	3,478
Short-term unearned revenue		7,225	6,514
Other		1,716	1,921
Total current liabilities		13,974	14,969
Long-term unearned revenue		1,790	1,663
Other long-term liabilities		1,056	932
Commitments and contingencies			
Stockholders' equity:			
Common stock and paid-in capital – shares authorized 24,000; outstanding 10,771 and 10,862		49,234	56,396
Retained earnings, including accumulated other comprehensive income of $1,840 and $1,119		15,678	18,429
Total stockholders' equity		64,912	74,825
Total liabilities and stockholders' equity	$	81,732	$ 92,389

	Dr.	Cr.
Inventories (A)	$7	
Accounts payable (L)		$7

LIABILITIES

Other Typical Current Liabilities

<u>Accrued compensation</u>: Wages owed to employees.

<u>Income taxes</u>: Taxes owed to IRS.

<u>Unearned revenues</u>: Revenue received for services not yet provided by the company. Examples include revenue from magazine subscriptions, gift certificates, airline tickets, hotel rental.

Microsoft 2004 Balance Sheet

Liabilities and stockholders' equity				
Current liabilities:				
Accounts payable	$	1,573	$	1,717
Accrued compensation		1,416		1,339
Income taxes		2,044		3,478
Short-term unearned revenue		7,225		6,514
Other		1,716		1,921
Total current liabilities		13,974		14,969
Long-term unearned revenue		1,790		1,663
Other long-term liabilities		1,056		932
Commitments and contingencies				
Stockholders' equity:				
Common stock and paid-in capital – shares authorized 24,000; outstanding 10,771 and 10,862		49,234		56,396
Retained earnings, including accumulated other comprehensive income of $1,840 and $1,119		15,678		18,429
Total stockholders' equity		64,912		74,825
Total liabilities and stockholders' equity	$	81,732	$	92,389

<u>Other</u>: A catch-all category that may include:
- ⇨ Dividends payable
- ⇨ Warranty costs
- ⇨ Litigation costs

<u>Notes payable</u>: Short term borrowings owed by the company that are due within 1 year.

<u>Current portion of long-term debt</u>: Portion of long-term debt which is due within 1 year.

⇨ Notice that the two liabilities (notes payable and current portion of long-term debt) above stem from financing activities, while all the previous current liabilities stemmed from operating activities.

⇨ This will prove an important distinction in the cash flow statement and in ratio analysis because cash used or generated from operating activities should be analyzed differently than cash used or generated from changes in debt financing.

LIABILITIES

Long-term debt is a long-term liability and often makes up a large share of a company's total liabilities.[1]

→ Companies with debt are committed to making fixed payments to their lenders.

→ Suppose you borrowed an additional $100 for your lemonade stand from the bank, which you will need to pay back in 10 years. In the meantime, you must make annual interest payments at a rate of 10%. Here is the impact of the original debt issuance:

	Dr.	Cr.
Cash (A)	$100	
Long-term debt (L)		$100

→ After the first year, you must make your first interest payment. Here is the impact on the financial statements:

	Dr.	Cr.
Interest Expense (SE)	$10	
Cash (A)		$10

[1] See Appendix 1 for more on debt

LIABILITIES

Capital leases represent long-term liabilities defined as contractual agreements, allowing a company to lease PP&E for a certain period of time in exchange for regular payments. Common leases involve cars and office/residential space.[1]

→ Although companies are leasing the equipment from someone, capital leases are treated as a purchase of PP&E on the balance sheet:

⇨ It is depreciated over its estimated useful life (asset side of B/S)

⇨ Lease payments are treated as debt obligations (liability)

Operating leases

Unlike capital leases, which treat the leased equipment as if it were a full purchase, operating leases are treated as if the company rented the PP&E, so operating lease payments are directly expensed on the income statement when they are incurred.

⇨ No asset is recorded on the balance sheet

⇨ No liability (lease obligations) is reported on the balance sheet

⇨ Operating leases represent a type of "off-balance sheet financing"

---

[1] See Appendix 2 for more on capital and operating leases

LIABILITIES

Deferred Taxes

→ The income tax expense that a company records on its income statement in accordance with GAAP does not always equal the taxes a company actually owes to the IRS.

→ For the purposes of reporting financial statements to the public (via the SEC), companies prepare their financial statements in accordance with U.S. GAAP. Companies trading in exchanges outside the U.S. may report in accordance with the GAAP of their respective countries. Under GAAP, tax expense is based on the GAAP pre-tax income.

→ However, in addition to reporting these financial statements, companies must also prepare financial statements to the IRS for filing tax returns.

→ The differences between GAAP tax expense and IRS taxes payable are recorded as deferred tax assets and liabilities.

Why do GAAP and IRS taxes differ?

2 major differences are revenue and depreciation assumptions

Revenue recognition
Scenario: a magazine collects subscription fees before sending out magazine to customers

GAAP	Subscription revenue is recognized when earned (i.e., when magazine is delivered).
IRS	Subscription fees are taxable as soon as they are received by magazine.

Depreciation assumptions:
Scenario: recording depreciation of fixed assets

GAAP	Management can choose from variety of depreciation methods (Straight-line, sum-of-the-years' digits, double-declining balance).
IRS	Company must record depreciation using the accelerated MACRS schedule.

LIABILITIES

Deferred Taxes

Figure 18. GAAP versus IRS Taxes

	GAAP	IRS	Reason for difference
Revenue	100	102	Different revenue recognition methods
COGS	20	20	
Depreciation & Amortization	10	17	MACRS vs. Straight-line Depreciation
Interest expense	5	5	
Statutory tax rate	35%	35%	
Pretax income (GAAP)	65		
Income tax expense (GAAP)	**22.75**		
Taxable income (IRS)		60	
Taxes payable (IRS)		**21**	
Net income	42.25	39	

LIABILITIES

A deferred tax liability is created and reported on the balance sheet when an income or expense item is treated differently on financial statements than it is on the company's tax returns, and that difference results in a greater tax expense on the financial statements than taxes payable on the tax return.

These differences are expected to reverse themselves (i.e. they are temporary differences) and to result in future cash outflows related to the payment of taxes.

	GAAP	IRS
Revenue	100	102
COGS	20	20
Depreciation & amortization	10	17
Interest expense	5	5
Statutory tax rate	35%	35%
Pretax income (GAAP)	65	
Income tax expense (GAAP)	**22.75**	
Taxable income (IRS)		60
Taxes payable (IRS)		**21**
Net Income	42.25	39

Income tax expense (GAAP)	$22.75
Less: Taxes payable (IRS)	(21.00)
Deferred tax liability (asset) created	$1.75

By far the most common way that deferred tax liabilities are created is when companies use an accelerated depreciation method (MACRS) in their tax returns and the straight-line method for financial reporting on the income statement. This treatment of depreciation almost always results in a deferred tax liability.

LIABILITIES

A deferred tax asset is created when taxes payable to the IRS are higher than those recorded on financial statements.

➔ Deferred tax assets therefore represent potential future tax savings.

➔ Some typical causes of deferred tax assets are warranty expenses and tax-loss carry forwards. In addition, restructuring and impairment charges generally result in a deferred tax asset.

⇨ The cost of restructuring is recognized on the income statement when restructuring is known, but is not expensed for tax purposes until the costs are actually paid.

⇨ The write-down of impaired assets is recognized for financial reporting, but not for tax purposes until the assets are sold.

⇨ Other expenses that generate deferred tax assets (or liabilities) include inventories due to different inventory accounting methods such as LIFO, FIFO, and average costs.

Deferred Taxes – Summary

➔ Notice that the differences between GAAP taxes and IRS taxes that create the deferred taxes are temporary: in our scenarios above, the magazine will not record subscriptions as revenues under GAAP until they are delivered – but they will eventually get delivered.

➔ Similarly, the company recorded higher depreciation under MACRS (IRS) of the initial years in the useful life of a fixed asset because it is an accelerated method (vs. straight-line depreciation), but in the latter years of the asset's useful life it will record a lower depreciation expense under MACRS than under straight-line depreciation.

➔ In the long run, the sum total of revenue recognized or depreciation recorded will be the same under GAAP and tax accounting. The annual differences we discussed thus represent temporary timing differences recorded as deferred tax assets and liabilities.

LIABILITIES

Minority Interest

Companies make frequent investments in other companies. Recall our earlier discussion of three accounting methods through which corporations record them:

1. Cost or Market method: Typically used for investments comprising less than 20% ownership stake in another business entity. These investments are represented on the balance sheet as an asset line item called *Investments in Securities*.

2. Equity method: Typically used for investments comprising a 20%-50% ownership interest in another company, recognizing a certain level of operational and strategic control. Represented on the balance sheet as an asset line item called *Investment in Affiliates*.

3. Consolidation method: Used for investments of greater than 50% in another business entity to reflect the investing company's virtually complete operational and strategic control of the entity.

    ⇨   All financial reports of these majority-owned investments are consolidated into the parent company's financial statements.

    ⇨   Note that even if a company does not own the entire subsidiary, but owns more than 50% of it, the company still consolidates all of the subsidiary's assets and liabilities.

    ⇨   The company accounts for the portion of the subsidiary that it does not own in a line item called *Minority Interest*.

LIABILITIES

Minority Interest

→ Companies that hold a majority ownership of more than 50% but less than 100% must account for minority interest they do not own.

→ Minority interest represents ownership by the subsidiary's shareholders which hold the remaining minority stake in the subsidiary.

ExxonMobil 2004 Balance Sheet

Liabilities			
Current liabilities			
Notes and loans payable	6	$ 3,280	$ 4,789
Accounts payable and accrued liabilities	6	31,763	28,445
Income taxes payable		7,938	5,152
Total current liabilities		$ 42,981	$ 38,386
Long-term debt	14	5,013	4,756
Annuity reserves	17	10,850	9,609
Accrued liabilities		6,279	5,283
Deferred income tax liabilities	19	21,092	20,118
Deferred credits and other long-term obligations		3,333	7,829
Equity of minority and preferred shareholders in affiliated companies		3,952	3,382
Total liabilities		$ 93,500	$ 84,363
Commitments and contingencies	16		
Shareholders' equity			
Benefit plan related balances		$ (1,014)	$ (634)
Common stock without par value (9,000 million shares authorized)		5,067	4,468
Earnings reinvested		134,390	115,956
Accumulated other nonowner changes in equity			
Cumulative foreign exchange translation adjustment		3,598	1,421
Minimum pension liability adjustment		(2,499)	(2,446)
Unrealized gains/(losses) on stock investments		428	511
Common stock held in treasury (1,618 million shares in 2004 and 1,451 million shares in 2003)		(38,214)	(29,361)
Total shareholders' equity		$101,756	$ 89,915
Total liabilities and shareholders' equity		$195,256	$174,278

Exercise: Minority Interest Created after an Acquisition

⇨ On January 1, 2004, Company A purchased 80% of Company B for $10 million.

⇨ What should Company A record under the "Minority Interest" account on the balance sheet?

LIABILITIES

Solution: Minority Interest Created After an Acquisition

⇨ Company A purchased 80% of Company B for $10 million, implying a total value of company B of $12.5. Accordingly, it must record $2.5 million (the remaining 20% it does not own) as minority interest.

Exercise: Minority Interest on the Income Statement

⇨ Let's return to the previous example. During 2004, Company B recorded earnings of $1 million and paid dividends of $250,000.

1. What should Company A record under the "Minority interest" account on the income statement as of 2004 year-end?

2. What should Company A record under the "Minority interest" account on the balance sheet as of 2004 year-end?

Solution: Minority Interest

---

1. Since Company A consolidates company B's entire income statement, but only owns 80% of it, it must expense the portion of the net income that it does not own as minority interest on the income statement, such that:

    ⇨   Company A records 20% * $1 million net income = $200,000 as a minority interest expense.

2. The minority interest balance on the liabilities side of the balance sheet increases by the $200,000 minority interest expense during the year, such that the total minority interest balance is now: $2.5 million + $0.2 million = $2.7 million.

    Since company B paid dividends of $250,000 which were also consolidated by company A, the portion of the dividends that is not "owned" by company A (20% * $250,000 = $50,000) should be netted out of the total minority interest balance, such that:

    ⇨   Minority interest as of 2004 year-end = $2.7 million - $0.05 million = $2.65 million.

BALANCE SHEET

SHAREHOLDERS' EQUITY

→ Recall that debt on the liabilities side of the balance sheet represents a major source of funds for companies.

→ Shareholders' Equity represents another major source of funds via:

1. Issuance of equity, and

2. Operations

Shareholders' equity typically consists of (but not always limited to):	
SHAREHOLDERS' EQUITY	
Preferred Stock	Stock that has special rights and takes priority over common stock
Common Stock Par Value	Par value of units of ownership of a corporation
Additional Paid-In Capital (APIC)	Represents capital received by a company when its shares are sold above their par value
Treasury Stock	Common stock that had been issued and then reacquired (bought back) by a company
Retained Earnings	Total amount of earnings of a company since its inception minus dividends and losses (if any)

BALANCE SHEET

SHAREHOLDERS' EQUITY

Introduction

→ Shareholders' equity (SE) represents monetary contributions of a company's equity (stock) owners, in addition to income from the course of operations.

→ Along with liabilities, SE forms another major source of funding for companies.

Microsoft 2004 Balance Sheet

Liabilities and stockholders' equity				
Current liabilities:				
Accounts payable	$	1,573	$	1,717
Accrued compensation		1,416		1,339
Income taxes		2,044		3,478
Short-term unearned revenue		7,225		6,514
Other		1,716		1,921
Total current liabilities		13,974		14,969
Long-term unearned revenue		1,790		1,663
Other long-term liabilities		1,056		932
Commitments and contingencies				
Stockholders' equity:				
Common stock and paid-in capital – shares authorized 24,000; outstanding 10,771 and 10,862		49,234		56,396
Retained earnings, including accumulated other comprehensive income of $1,840 and $1,119		15,678		18,429
Total stockholders' equity		64,912		74,825
Total liabilities and stockholders' equity	$	81,732	$	92,389

→ Represents the residual value (net worth) of assets by the shareholders following the repayment of liabilities: Assets – Liabilities = SE

→ SE usually consists of:
  ⇨ Capital Stock
  ⇨ Additional Paid-In Capital
  ⇨ Treasury Stock
  ⇨ Retained Earnings

BALANCE SHEET

SHAREHOLDERS' EQUITY

Capital Stock

➜ One way companies choose to raise money (for growth, acquisitions, etc.) is through the sale (issuance) of its shares of stock.

➜ Each share of stock represents a fractional ownership in companies, allowing people who purchased them to become (on a small scale) corporate owners i.e. shareholders.

Common Stock: Fractional unit of equity ownership in companies

⇨ Issued shares of common stock are recorded at their nominal (fractional or par) value

⇨ Ex: $0.10/share, $0.50/share
⇨ Par value is NOT market value of shares (share price)

Preferred Stock: Takes priority over common stock and has special rights such as:

⇨ Priority over regular stock relating to dividends
⇨ Possible conversion into common stock at a pre-set exchange rate
⇨ Possible retirement/redemption at the option of a company
⇨ Priority over regular stock relating to claims of assets in case of liquidation

SHAREHOLDERS' EQUITY

Additional Paid-In Capital (APIC)

→ APIC represents capital received by a company when its shares are sold <u>above</u> their par value.

→ When a company issues shares, two entries in the shareholders' equity section take place:
  1. Common stock (Par Value) and
  2. APIC

Microsoft 2004 Balance Sheet

Liabilities and stockholders' equity			
Current liabilities:			
Accounts payable	$	1,573	$ 1,717
Accrued compensation		1,416	1,339
Income taxes		2,044	3,478
Short-term unearned revenue		7,225	6,514
Other		1,716	1,921
Total current liabilities		13,974	14,969
Long-term unearned revenue		1,790	1,663
Other long-term liabilities		1,056	932
Commitments and contingencies			
Stockholders' equity:			
Common stock and paid-in capital – shares authorized 24,000; outstanding 10,771 and 10,862		49,234	56,396
Retained earnings, including accumulated other comprehensive income of $1,840 and $1,119		15,678	18,429
Total stockholders' equity		64,912	74,825
Total liabilities and stockholders' equity	$	81,732	$ 92,389

Suppose a company issues 1 million shares with par value of $0.10 per share for net proceeds of $20 million. What is the impact on the financial statements?

1. Common stock total value: 1 million shares x $0.10/share = $100,000

2. APIC: $20 million – $100,000 = $19.9 million

3. Cash: $20 million

	Debits	Credits
Cash	$20 million	
Common Stock		$0.1 million
APIC		$19.9 million

SHAREHOLDERS' EQUITY

Treasury Stock

➜ Common stock that had been issued and then reacquired (bought back) by a company:

> **No. of Outstanding Shares = Shares Issued – Treasury Stock**

➜ Treasury stock is a negative (contra) account

Companies repurchase stock for various reasons:

➜ To boost EPS (repurchase of shares reduces total shares outstanding – above equation).

➜ To change the company's capital structure (more debt/less equity).

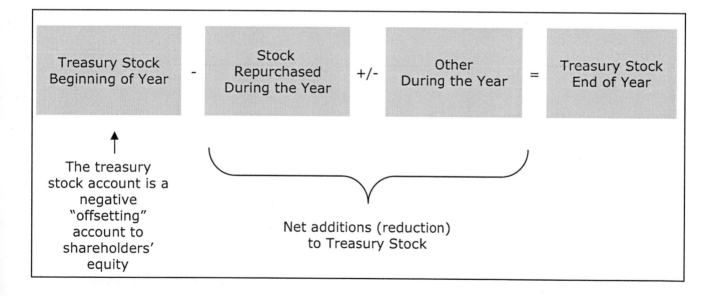

SHAREHOLDERS' EQUITY

Retained Earnings

➔ Cumulative earnings (net of dividends) over a company's entire existence, which have been withheld within the firm and not distributed to the shareholders.

➔ Serves as an important link between the balance sheet and the income statement, allowing net income every year to flow through to the balance sheet.

Retained Earnings =
(Net Income - Dividends)$_1$
+ (Net Income - Dividends)$_2$
+ (Net Income - Dividends)$_3$
+ . . .
+ (Net Income - Dividends)$_t$

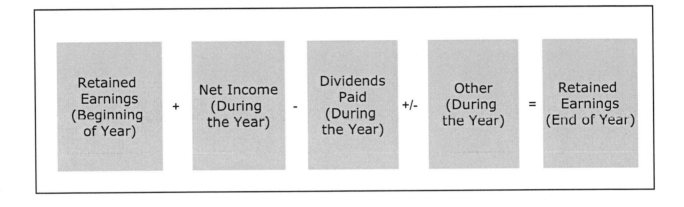

Retained Earnings (Beginning of Year) + Net Income (During the Year) - Dividends Paid (During the Year) +/- Other (During the Year) = Retained Earnings (End of Year)

CHAPTER 7

CASH FLOW STATEMENT

CASH FLOW STATEMENT

INTRODUCTION

➔ Recall the structure of the income statement – the final measure of profitability after the deduction of all expenses is net income.

➔ Net income is extremely useful metric in financial analysis – it reflects on-going profitability.

➔ However, the income statement has a significant limitation – accrual accounting.

The Lemonade Stand – Revisited

⇨ You purchased a lemon squeezer and a lemonade stand for $30 and estimated that both of these fixed assets will have a useful life of 3 years, by the end of which they will be obsolete and be thrown away.

⇨ It is important to recall that even though you paid cash upfront for the entire cost of the machine, you did not expense the entire $30 cost on the income statement.

⇨ Instead, you estimated a useful life of the squeezer for generating lemonade (i.e. revenues for your business) to be 3 years, and so you spread the depreciation expense (at $10 per year) over this period in order to match revenues and expenses, as required by the accrual accounting.

January 1, 2004 to December 31, 2004

Income Statement	
Revenues	100
- Cost of Goods Sold	20
- SG&A	15
- D&A	10
EBIT	55
- Interest Expense	5
- Taxes	20
Net Income	30

INTRODUCTION

Year 1
⇨ D&A expense was $10 (as shown on the right)
⇨ Actual cash expense was $30

Year 2
⇨ D&A expense is $10
⇨ Cash expense is $0 – you already paid for the machine in year 1

Year 3
⇨ D&A expense is $10
⇨ Cash expense is $0

	Year 1	Year 2	Year 3
Cash	$30	-	-
D&A	$10	$10	$10

➔ Clearly the cash flowing out of the company does not equal the expenses that the company has recorded on the income statement.

➔ Also recall from a previous example in which you sold some lemonade on credit. You recorded the sale as revenues on the income statement, even though you didn't actually receive cash income from the transaction until some time later.

➔ It should be clear by now that the income statement, which by virtue of employing the accrual method of accounting, is quite helpful in many respects, has by definition the limitation of not being able to show us exactly what is happening to a company's cash flows for that specific accounting period.

CASH FLOW STATEMENT

INTRODUCTION

Why is tracking a company's cash flows important? Let's imagine two opposite scenarios:

Scenario 1
⇨   Company A shows a very profitable income statement, but is losing cash. You would definitely want to analyze why, particularly if that company has few cash reserves, but a large amount of debt outstanding that it must repay to its lenders in the near future, but may be unable to do so.

⇨   Possible reason: the company may be selling more products on credit.

Scenario 2
⇨   Company B shows negative profitability, but is accumulating a very large amount of cash. What is the source of that cash and is it sustainable at current levels?

⇨   Possible reason: Suppliers have eased payment terms or the company has reduced purchases of fixed assets abruptly.

The cash flow statement has been created for the purpose of being able to trace the company's cash flows and their sources/uses.

CASH FLOW STATEMENT

INTRODUCTION

Cash Flow Statement To the Rescue!

→ The cash flow statement reconciles net income to a company's actual change in cash balance over a period in time (quarter or year).

→ It is a line-by-line reconciliation, starting with net income and ending with total change in cash balance.

→ Along with the income statement and the balance sheet, the cash flow statement is required by the SEC.

⇨ Unlike the income statement, whose primary purpose is to present a company's operating performance, the major purpose of the cash flow statement is to record a company's uses and sources of cash.

⇨ The cash flow statement has become increasingly important for the purposes of financial analysis. Why?

⇨ Income statement and balance sheet can be manipulated through the use of different accounting methods and assumptions.

⇨ However, a company's uses and sources of cash are objectively recorded when cash is paid and received, respectively.

Cash inflows / outflows are segregated into three major categories:

1. Cash Flow from Operations

2. Cash Flow from Investing

3. Cash Flow from Financing

INTRODUCTION

STANDARD LINE ITEMS IN CASH FLOW STATEMENT (INDIRECT METHOD)

Net Income	Starting point of Cash Flow Statement
Plus: Depreciation and amortization	Add back non-cash D&A expense
Plus: Increase in accounts payable	Add back reported expenses not actually paid in cash
Plus: Increase in other current operating liabilities (non-debt)	Add back reported expenses not actually paid in cash (deferred liabilities, etc.)
Less: Increase in accounts receivable	Deduct reported revenues not received in cash
Less: Increase in inventories	Deduct amounts paid in cash to buy inventories but not counted as COGS
Less: Increase in all other current assets (except cash)	Varies
Less: Gain on sale of assets	Deduct gains reported in net income that are part of investing cash flow
= **CASH FLOW FROM OPERATIONS**	Usually a positive number
Plus: Proceeds from sale of long-term assets and investments	Cash inflow that includes gain (loss) on the sale of asset or investment
Less: Capital expenditures	Outlays for PP&E and other investments
Less: Increase in all other long-term assets	
= **CASH FLOW FROM INVESTING ACTIVITIES**	Usually a negative number
Plus: Increase in bank loans	Net capital raised from negotiated debt
Plus: Increase in long-term debt	
Plus: Increase in preferred stock	Net capital raised from issuing new preferred and common shares
Plus: Increase in common stock	
Plus: Increase in paid-in-capital	
Less: Increase in treasury stock	
Less: Dividends paid	Payments to preferred and common shareholders
= **CASH FLOW FROM FINANCING ACTIVITIES**	Can be either positive or negative depending on whether debt was raised or paid down
INCREASE IN CASH AND CASH EQUIVALENTS	Must agree with the net change in cash and cash equivalents on the balance sheet

CASH FLOW STATEMENT

INTRODUCTION

The cash flow statement is presented as follows:

1. Cash Flow from Operations

+

2. Cash Flow from Investing

+

3. Cash Flow from Financing

=

Net Increase in Cash during Year

+

Cash at Beginning of Year

=

Cash at End of Year

Microsoft 2004 Cash Flow Statement

CONSOLIDATED STATEMENT OF CASH FLOWS

(millions of dollars)

	Note Reference Number	2004	2003	2002
Cash flows from operating activities				
Net income				
Accruing to ExxonMobil shareholders		$ 25,330	$ 21,510	$ 11,460
Accruing to minority and preferred interests		776	694	209
Cumulative effect of accounting change, net of income tax		—	(550)	—
Adjustments for noncash transactions				
Depreciation and depletion		9,767	9,047	8,310
Deferred income tax charges/(credits)		(1,134)	1,827	297
Annuity provisions		886	(1,489)	(500)
Accrued liability provisions		806	264	(90)
Dividends received greater than/(less than) equity in current earnings of equity companies		(1,643)	(402)	(170)
Changes in operational working capital, excluding cash and debt				
Reduction/(increase) – Notes and accounts receivable		(472)	(1,286)	(305)
– Inventories		(223)	(100)	353
– Prepaid taxes and expenses		11	42	32
Increase/(reduction) – Accounts and other payables		6,333	1,130	365
Ruhrgas transaction	5	—	(2,240)	1,466
All other items – net		114	51	(150)
Net cash provided by operating activities		$ 40,551	$ 28,498	$ 21,268
Cash flows from investing activities				
Additions to property, plant and equipment		$(11,986)	$(12,859)	$(11,437)
Sales of subsidiaries, investments and property, plant and equipment	5	2,754	2,290	2,793
Increase in restricted cash and cash equivalents	4,16	(4,604)	—	—
Additional investments and advances		(2,287)	(809)	(2,012)
Collection of advances		1,213	536	898
Net cash used in investing activities		$(14,910)	$(10,842)	$ (9,758)
Cash flows from financing activities				
Additions to long-term debt		$ 470	$ 127	$ 396
Reductions in long-term debt		(562)	(914)	(246)
Additions to short-term debt		450	715	751
Reductions in short-term debt		(2,243)	(1,730)	(927)
Additions/(reductions) in debt with less than 90-day maturity		(66)	(322)	(281)
Cash dividends to ExxonMobil shareholders		(6,896)	(6,515)	(6,217)
Cash dividends to minority interests		(215)	(430)	(169)
Changes in minority interests and sales/(purchases) of affiliate stock		(215)	(247)	(161)
Common stock acquired		(9,951)	(5,881)	(4,798)
Common stock sold		960	434	299
Net cash used in financing activities		$(18,268)	$(14,763)	$(11,353)
Effects of exchange rate changes on cash		$ 532	$ 504	$ 525
Increase/(decrease) in cash and cash equivalents		$ 7,905	$ 3,397	$ 682
Cash and cash equivalents at beginning of year		10,626	7,229	6,547
Cash and cash equivalents at end of year		$ 18,531	$ 10,626	$ 7,229

CASH FLOW FROM OPERATIONS

→ The starting point of the cash flow from operations section is Net Income.

→ Recall that net income depicts a company's profitability arising from its daily operations, while cash flow from operations attempts to capture cash movement associated with these daily activities.

→ Net income therefore is a "natural" starting point of the cash flow from operations section.

→ After net income (the first line in the cash flow statement), the remaining line items determining cash from operations reflect adjustments that need to be made in order to reconcile net income to actual cash generated from operations.

Microsoft 2004 Cash Flow Statement

CONSOLIDATED STATEMENT OF CASH FLOWS

	Note Reference Number	2004	2003	2002
		(millions of dollars)		
Cash flows from operating activities				
Net income				
Accruing to ExxonMobil shareholders		$ 25,330	$ 21,510	$ 11,460
Accruing to minority and preferred interests		776	694	209
Cumulative effect of accounting change, net of income tax		—	(550)	—
Adjustments for noncash transactions				
Depreciation and depletion		9,767	9,047	8,310
Deferred income tax charges/(credits)		(1,134)	1,827	297
Annuity provisions		886	(1,489)	(500)
Accrued liability provisions		806	264	(90)
Dividends received greater than/(less than) equity in current earnings of equity companies		(1,643)	(402)	(170)
Changes in operational working capital, excluding cash and debt				
Reduction/(increase) – Notes and accounts receivable		(472)	(1,286)	(305)
– Inventories		(223)	(100)	353
– Prepaid taxes and expenses		11	42	32
Increase/(reduction) – Accounts and other payables		6,333	1,130	365
Ruhrgas transaction	5	—	(2,240)	1,466
All other items – net		114	51	(159)
Net cash provided by operating activities		$ 40,551	$ 28,498	$ 21,268
Cash flows from investing activities				
Additions to property, plant and equipment		$(11,986)	$(12,859)	$(11,437)
Sales of subsidiaries, investments and property, plant and equipment	5	2,754	2,290	2,793
Increase in restricted cash and cash equivalents	4,16	(4,604)	—	—
Additional investments and advances		(2,287)	(809)	(2,012)
Collection of advances		1,213	536	898
Net cash used in investing activities		$(14,910)	$(10,842)	$ (9,758)
Cash flows from financing activities				
Additions to long-term debt		$ 470	$ 127	$ 396
Reductions in long-term debt		(562)	(914)	(246)
Additions to short-term debt		450	715	751
Reductions in short-term debt		(2,243)	(1,730)	(927)
Additions/(reductions) in debt with less than 90-day maturity		(66)	(322)	(281)
Cash dividends to ExxonMobil shareholders		(6,896)	(6,515)	(6,217)
Cash dividends to minority interests		(215)	(430)	(169)
Changes in minority interests and sales/(purchases) of affiliate stock		(215)	(247)	(161)
Common stock acquired		(9,951)	(5,881)	(4,798)
Common stock sold		960	434	299
Net cash used in financing activities		$(18,268)	$(14,763)	$(11,353)
Effects of exchange rate changes on cash		$ 532	$ 504	$ 525
Increase/(decrease) in cash and cash equivalents		$ 7,905	$ 3,397	$ 682
Cash and cash equivalents at beginning of year		10,626	7,229	6,547
Cash and cash equivalents at end of year		$ 18,531	$ 10,626	$ 7,229

CASH FLOW FROM OPERATIONS

➔ Typically, three major "non-cash" adjustments made in the cash flow from operations section include:

    1. <u>Depreciation</u>
- ⇨ As the lemonade stand case showed, depreciation expense simply allocates the costs of the original purchase of fixed assets over their useful lives.

- ⇨ Depreciation expense therefore does not depict any actual cash outflow (payment) and must therefore be added back to net income.

    2. <u>Increases / decreases in deferred taxes</u>
- ⇨ Typically companies are able to defer paying some portion of the income tax expense shown on their income statement. Accordingly, these deferred taxes, which have not been paid out in cash, must be added back to net income on the cash flow statement.

    3. <u>Changes in working capital</u>
- ⇨ Introduced on the next page

CASH FLOW STATEMENT

CASH FLOW FROM OPERATIONS

Working capital

→ Recall from the balance sheet that current assets represent assets that can be converted into cash within 1 year, while current liabilities represent obligations due within 1 year.

→ Working capital, calculated as current assets less current liabilities, is an important measure of a company's ability to cover day-to-day operating activities.

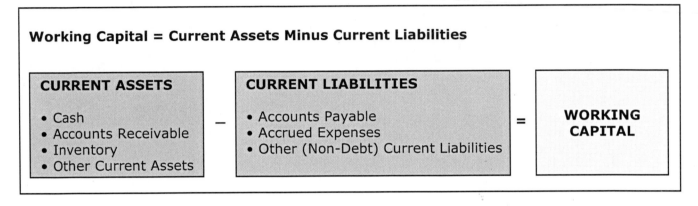

Working Capital = Current Assets Minus Current Liabilities

CURRENT ASSETS	CURRENT LIABILITIES	WORKING CAPITAL
• Cash • Accounts Receivable • Inventory • Other Current Assets	• Accounts Payable • Accrued Expenses • Other (Non-Debt) Current Liabilities	

(CURRENT ASSETS − CURRENT LIABILITIES = WORKING CAPITAL)

→ In addition to adding back depreciation expense and any increases in deferred tax liabilities in order to reconcile GAAP net income to cash from operations, we must also incorporate changes in working capital (excluding changes in cash and short-term debt).

⇨ The cash flow statement is a reconciliation of what happens to cash during a reported period.

⇨ If working capital balances changed from one year to the next, there is a corresponding cash impact that must be represented on the cash flow statement.

CASH FLOW FROM OPERATIONS

Working capital items reflect balances on the balance sheet:

➜ Company ABC has an accounts receivable balance of $200m in 2002. That means that company ABC expects to receive $200m that it is owed by customers.

➜ What if the following year (2003), ABC expects accounts receivable to decline to a balance of $150m?

➜ Essentially, it means that ABC expects that $50m of the $200m they are owed from customers will be paid to them by those customers.

➜ That means that ABC's cash balance will go up by $50m (remember, since the accounts receivable balance declines, that implies that ABC is receiving money from the customers who originally purchased its goods or services on credit).

➜ Recall that accounts receivable is a current asset (CA); the converse cash impact happens with current liabilities (CL) – when accounts payable or accrued expenses are expected to go down by $50m from one year to the next, it implies that the company paid off $50m that they owed to vendors – that is a drain on cash.

CASH FLOW FROM OPERATIONS

Exercise: Working Capital

---

1. What was the change in working capital (excluding cash) during 2004?

2. Was the change in working capital a source or a use of cash for the lemonade stand?

January 1, 2004

Balance Sheet	
Assets	
Cash	100
Accounts Receivable	0
Inventories	20
PP&E	30
Total Assets	150
Liabilities	
Accounts Payable	0
Debt	50
Total Liabilities	50
Shareholders' Equity	
Common Stock and APIC	100
Retained Earnings	0
Total SE	100

December 31, 2004

Balance Sheet	
Assets	
Cash	160
Accounts Receivable	0
Inventories	0
PP&E	20
Total Assets	180
Liabilities	
Accounts Payable	0
Debt	50
Total Liabilities	50
Shareholders' Equity	
Common Stock & APIC	100
Retained Earnings	30
Total SE	130

CASH FLOW FROM OPERATIONS

Solution: Working Capital

1. Working capital (excluding cash) increased by $20 during 2004 from $0 to $20.

2. Accounts receivable increased by $20 during the year. The implication is that more people paid on credit during the year, which represents a drain on cash for the company, as some of the revenues that came in during the year increased the accounts receivable balance instead of cash.

BOTTOM LINE:

⮑ When working capital assets increase, the cash impact is negative.

⮑ Conversely, when working capital liabilities increase, the cash impact is positive.

CASH FLOW STATEMENT

CASH FLOW FROM INVESTING ACTIVITIES

➔ The Cash Flows from Investing Activities section of the cash flow statement tracks additions and reductions to fixed assets and investments during the year (corresponding to the long-term asset side of the balance sheet).

➔ Several accounts are typically found in the investing cash flow section:

⇨ Capital expenditures: Organic expansion of fixed assets (cash outflow)

⇨ Acquisitions: Purchased fixed assets (cash outflow)

⇨ Asset sales: Disposal of fixed assets (cash inflow)

⇨ Purchases of investments: Acquisition of debt/equity securities (cash outflow)

⇨ Sales of investments: Disposal of debt/equity securities (cash inflow)

CASH FLOW FROM FINANCING ACTIVITIES

➔ The Cash Flows from Financing Activities section of the cash flow statement tracks changes in the company's sources of debt and equity financing (corresponding to the liabilities and shareholders' equity side of the balance sheet).

➔ Several accounts are typically found in the financing cash flow section:

⇨ Issuance of debt: Increase in the level of borrowings (cash inflow)

⇨ Repayment of debt: Decrease in the level of borrowings (cash outflow)

⇨ Common stock issued: Issuance of equity (common stock – cash inflow)

⇨ Common stock repurchased: Repurchase of equity (treasury stock – cash outflow)

⇨ Payment of dividends: Distribution of cash (cash outflow)

HOW THE CASH FLOW IS LINKED TO THE BALANCE SHEET

> **The change in cash reflected on CFS must always equal the change in cash reported on the balance sheet between two periods**

In the lemonade stand example:

Change in cash (Balance Sheet)	=	Change in cash (Cash Flow Statement)
$60	=	$60

January 1, 2004

Balance Sheet

Assets

Cash	100
Accounts Receivable	0
Inventories	20
PP&E	30
Total Assets	150

Liabilities

Accounts Payable	0
Debt	50
Total Liabilities	50

Shareholders' Equity

Common Stock and APIC	100
Retained Earnings	0
Total SE	100

December 31, 2004

Balance Sheet

Assets

Cash	160
Accounts Receivable	0
Inventories	0
PP&E	20
Total Assets	180

Liabilities

Accounts Payable	0
Debt	50
Total Liabilities	50

Shareholders' Equity

Common Stock & APIC	100
Retained Earnings	30
Total SE	130

January 1–December 31, 2004

Cash Flow Statement

Net Income	30
+ D&A	10
+ Decrease in inventories	20
+ Decrease in A/R	0
+ Increase in A/P	0
Cash Flow from Operations	**60**
- Capital expenditures	0
Cash flow from investing	**0**
Increase in bank loans	0
Common stock	0
Dividends	0
Cash flow from financing	**0**
Change in cash	**60**
Cash – beginning of 2004	100
Cash – end of 2004	160

HOW THE CASH FLOW IS LINKED TO THE BALANCE SHEET

→ **FINAL EXERCISE**

⇨ Please log on to
www.wallstreetprep.com/accounting.html

⇨ Download and save the Excel file titled: "Final
Accounting Exercise"

⇨ Complete the exercise

CHAPTER 8

FINANCIAL RATIO ANALYSIS

FINANCIAL RATIO ANALYSIS

INTRODUCTION

What is Financial Ratio Analysis?

➔ Ratios express a mathematical relationship between two quantities and can appear in the form of a:

- ⇨ Percentage (%)
- ⇨ Rate (greater than, equal to, less than)
- ⇨ Proportion (numerator / denominator)

➔ Financial ratio analysis (often referred to as ratio analysis) utilizes ratios and relationships between various financial statement accounts as basic tools to compare operational, financial, and investing performance of companies over time and against one another.

Drawbacks of Financial Ratio Analysis

- ➲ Although ratio analysis is extremely useful and is a fundamental component of financial analysis, analysts must recognize that it does come with some limitations.

- ➲ Conclusions derived from ratio analysis are often based on the users' intentions and frame of reference i.e. "interpretation depends on the user."

- ➲ Ratio computation is derived from financial reports, which are issued only at specific intervals (10-K – annually; 10-Q – quarterly), allowing for ratio analysis only at specific points in time rather than on a "continuous" basis.

- ➲ Ratios do not take into account differences between industries and various accounting methods.

FINANCIAL RATIO ANALYSIS

CLASSIFICATION

Ratios are often classified into four categories:

RATIO ANALYSIS			
Category	**Liquidity Ratios**	**Profitability Ratios**	**Activity Ratios**	**Solvency Ratios (Coverage)**
Purpose	Measure of a firm's short-term ability to meet its current obligations	Measure of a firm's profitability relative to its assets (operating efficiency) and to its revenues (operating profitability)	Measure of efficiency of a firm's assets	Measure of a firm's ability to repay its debt obligations
Example	Current ratio	Gross margin Operating margin Profit margin EPS	Inventory turnover Receivables turnover Payables turnover Asset turnover	Debt to total capital Debt to equity Debt to EBITDA Debt to int. expense

FINANCIAL RATIO ANALYSIS

CALCULATIONS

CATEGORIES OF RATIO ANALYSIS	FORMULA	A MEASURE OF:
LIQUIDITY		
Current ratio	Current assets / Current liabilities	Short-term debt-paying ability
Quick (acid) test	Cash + accounts receivable / Current liabilities	Immediate short-term ability
Current cash debt coverage ratio	Cash from operating activities / Average current liabilities	A company's ability to pay off its current liabilities with cash from operations
ACTIVITY		
Receivable turnover	Net sales / Average accounts receivable	Liquidity of receivables
Inventory turnover	Cost of good sold / Average inventory	Liquidity of inventories
Asset turnover	Net sales / Average total assets	Efficiency of assets to generate sales
PROFITABILITY		
Profit margin on sales	Net income / Net sales	Net income generated by sales
Rate of return on assets (ROA)	Net income / Average total assets	Profitability of assets
Rate of return on common stock equity	Net income to common stockholders / Average common shareholders' equity	Profitability of shareholders' investment
Earnings per share (EPS)	Net income to common stockholders / Weighted average shares outstanding	Net income earned on each share of common stock
Price earnings ratio (P/E)	Market price of stock / Earnings per share	Market price per share to EPS
Payout ratio	Cash dividends / Net income	Percentage of earnings distributed in the form of cash dividends
COVERAGE		
Debt to total assets	Total debt / Total assets	Percentage of total assets provided by creditors
Times interest earned	EBIT / Interest expense	Ability to meet interest payments when they are due
Cash debt coverage ratio	Cash from operating activities / Average total liabilities	A company's ability to repay its total liabilities with cash from operations
Book value per share	Common shareholders' equity / Outstanding shares	"Liquidation" value of each share

CHAPTER 9

 **APPENDIX**

Recall that in our lemonade stand example, you borrowed some money from a bank and put in some of your own money to get started. What you borrowed represents debt and your own money (as the sole shareholder in your lemonade stand business) represents your shareholders' equity.

Debt and shareholders' equity are regarded as the primary sources of funding (capital) for all corporations.

How are these two forms of capital raised?

Corporations looking to raise capital (i.e. get money) can issue securities (debt or equity) in the capital markets.

Investment banks serve as financial intermediaries, helping these firms to raise capital by offering these securities to a broad range of institutional (mutual funds, hedge funds, pensions) and individual investors.

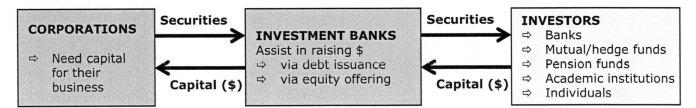

Debt and equity serve as primary sources of funding for corporations:

	SOURCES OF FUNDING		
Type of capital	**DEBT**	**EQUITY**	
Type of securities	**Fixed-Income Securities**	**Common Stock**	**Preferred Stock**
Who issues securities	Governments Federal Agencies **Corporations**	**Corporations**	

Who issues debt?

While our focus is on corporate debt (issued by companies), note that issuers of debt include local, state and federal governments as well as various federal agencies.

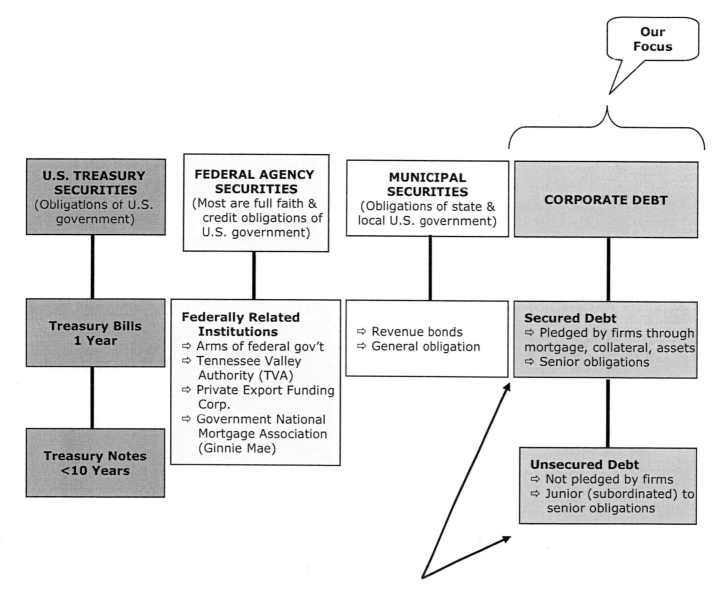

Seniority level of corporate debt varies

APPENDIX 1

Long-term debt

→ Some long-term debt has higher priority than other debt over claims in the event of bankruptcy.

→ Such debt is called senior debt, while debt with lower priority is called subordinated debt.

→ Debt generally has a number of restrictions (called covenants) that provide protection for both lenders and borrowers.

→ These covenants appear in the indenture (debt agreement) and may include:

⇨ Interest rate and amount of the issued debt
⇨ Provisions for the repayment of debt
⇨ Restrictions on the amount and type of additional debt that can be issued
⇨ Dividend restrictions
⇨ Minimum level of operating performance that must be met over a certain period in order to meet debt covenants

Capital vs. Operating Leases

As previously discussed, there is an important difference between how capital leases and operating leases are accounted for. So how do companies determine when to classify leases as capital or operating?

Any of the four criteria must be met for a lease to be capitalized by a lessee:

1. Title to a leased property/plant/equipment is expected to be transferred to a lessee at the end of the lease.

2. A bargain purchase option exists – a lessee can purchase the leased property at below fair market value during the lease.

3. The lease exceeds 75% of the asset's estimated economic life.

4. The present value of the minimum lease payments incurred by a lessee is 90% or greater of the leased asset's fair value.

➔ For operating leases, lessees are required to disclose minimum annual lease payments for at least the next five years:

Microsoft 2004 10-K

We have operating leases for most U.S. and international sales and support offices and certain equipment. Rental expense for operating leases was $318 million, $290 million, and $331 million in fiscal 2002, 2003, and 2004, respectively. Future minimum rental commitments under noncancellable leases, in millions of dollars, are as follows:

(In millions) Year Ended June 30	Amount
2005	$ 148
2006	124
2007	81
2008	62
2009 and thereafter	120
	$ 535

APPENDIX 2

For a lessor to capitalize a lease:

➜ Any of the aforementioned four criteria applicable to a lessee must be met; and

➜ A lessor must be reasonably assured of collecting minimum lease payments from a lessee; and

➜ A lessor's performance is virtually complete and future costs relating to the leased asset can be reasonably estimated.

The lessor cannot capitalize a lease if the lessee recognizes it as an operating lease